Moufflet

More Than
100 GOURMET MUFFIN RECIPES
That Rise to Any Occasion

641.8157
JAG

KELLY JAGGERS, author of *Not-So-Humble Pies*

Adamsmedia

Avon, Massachusetts

Published by
Adams Media, a division of F+W Media, Inc.
57 Littlefield Street, Avon, MA 02322. U.S.A.
www.adamsmedia.com

ISBN 10: 1-4405-3892-1
ISBN 13: 978-1-4405-3892-6
eISBN 10: 1-4405-4070-5
eISBN 13: 978-1-4405-4070-7

Printed in China.

10   9   8   7   6   5   4   3   2   1

Library of Congress Cataloging-in-Publication Data
Jaggers, Kelly.
  Moufflet / Kelly Jaggers.
      p. cm.
  Includes index.
  ISBN 978-1-4405-3892-6 (hardcover) – ISBN 1-4405-3892-1 (hardcover) – ISBN 978-
1-4405-4070-7 (ebook) – ISBN 1-4405-4070-5 (ebook)
  1. Muffins. I. Title.
  TX770.M83J34 2012
  641.81'57–dc23

                          2012014510

Always follow safety and commonsense cooking protocol while using kitchen utensils, operating ovens and stoves, and handling uncooked food. If children are assisting in the preparation of any recipe, they should always be supervised by an adult.

This publication is designed to provide accurate and authoritative information with regard to the subject matter covered. It is sold with the understanding that the publisher is not engaged in rendering legal, accounting, or other professional advice. If legal advice or other expert assistance is required, the services of a competent professional person should be sought.
—From a *Declaration of Principles* jointly adopted by a Committee of the American Bar Association and a Committee of Publishers and Associations

Many of the designations used by manufacturers and sellers to distinguish their product are claimed as trademarks. Where those designations appear in this book and Adams Media was aware of a trademark claim, the designations have been printed with initial capital letters.

Images courtesy of Kelly Jaggers. Line art on recipe pages © istockphoto.com/azureforest.

This book is available at quantity discounts for bulk purchases.
For information, please call 1-800-289-0963.

Dedication

This book is dedicated to my men: Mark, Howard, Pete, Wayne, and Mike. I am lucky to have you all in my life.

Acknowledgments

First I would like to thank all the people who made this book possible, and made it look so darn good! Erin Dawson, Deb Baker, your hard work is so very appreciated! Again, thank you to my editor, Katie Corcoran Lytle. You are a joy to work with, and I could not have done it without you!

I am blessed with an amazing support network that is willing, among other things, to test recipes for me even though they do not have to. To Sandra and Joshua, thank you for taking your Sunday out to test for me. It was so appreciated and your help could not have come at a better time! I again owe my mother, Carol, for just absolutely everything, but specifically for taking what little free time you had to test recipes. You are amazing!

To my father, Howard, who has been put through the wringer over the last year. You did it with more humor than I could ever muster. You are loved.

Finally, to Mark, I just want to say thank you for keeping me company while I worked, for reminding me that I am only human, and for forcing me to take a break once in a while.

Contents

PART 2: **Savory Sensations** 87

CHAPTER 3: **Brunch, Lunch, and Dinner Muffins** 89

CHAPTER 4: **Savory, Spicy, and a Little Sweet** 121

PART 3: To Top It Off   151

CHAPTER 5:
Sensational Spreads   153

CHAPTER 6:
Crumbles and Glazes   171

Introduction

Candied pecans. Stone-ground cornmeal. Pomegranate molasses.

Gone are the days of boring old blueberry and plain old corn muffins! Today's melt-in-your-mouth muffins—or *moufflets* as they call them in France—are packed with exotic spices and unique flavors that make any occasion and any time of day upscale and sophisticated. Whether sweet or savory suits your fancy, these new gourmet muffin creations are sure to please your palate.

Muffins are like individual servings of pure, delicious comfort. Fresh from the oven or enjoyed on the go, they are a treat that simply cannot be beat. What makes muffins even better is how easy they are to create at home. These bakery-fresh pastries take mere moments to mix, and are a perfect canvas for experimenting with new flavors and ingredients. It is a snap to transform a muffin from simple to simply amazing with only a few special ingredients like specialty cheeses and spicy peppers or exotic dried fruits and even candy. In a fraction of the time it takes to make most other kinds of bread you can have an exciting, flavorful tray of piping hot muffins ready for most any occasion!

Of course, there is more to the muffin than just the muffin itself. You can dress up your creations with luscious spreads, flavored butters, sweet glazes, and crumbly toppings that incorporate unexpected ingredients and add a little pizzazz to your muffins. Spreads are versatile. They can be used on sweet and savory muffins to suit any taste. You can even make a few different spreads and invite your friends and family to mix and match their own special blend. In addition, an otherwise plain batch of muffins is easily dressed up with a golden, buttery crumble, a nutty oat topping, or a drizzle of a sweet glaze. These recipes add extra layers of texture and flavor, and will make your muffins as beautiful to look at as they are to devour.

Whether you choose sweet, savory, or a little bit of both, you cannot go wrong with these upscale recipes. Not only are they yummy but they are an easy way to show the people you bake them for how much you care. What better way to treat overnight guests than with a basket of warm muffins and some delicious spreads? Or, how better to top off a comforting dinner than with some fresh, savory muffins? Muffins are made to be enjoyed, either alone or with friends, and with these exciting recipes, the muffins you will bake will be anything but boring!

How to Make a Muffin

Muffins are unique because of the aptly named Muffin Method that is used to make them. And with just three steps this method is very easy to master:

○ First, sift together the dry ingredients, including the sugar; then in a separate bowl whisk together the wet ingredients.

○ Second, pour the wet ingredients into the dry and mix until the dry ingredients are just moistened; about 10–12 strokes will do it. The batter will be lumpy, but lumps are your friend. Despite how odd it may feel to have lumps in the batter, the lumps are the key to tender, airy muffins. If the recipe calls for additions, such as nuts, chocolate chips, or diced fruit, give the batter about 10 strokes to get things mostly combined, add the additional ingredients, and then give the batter about 2 or 3 more strokes to finish. Remember, you want the ingredients combined, but the less you mix the better.

○ Finally, just scoop the batter into a standard 12-cup muffin pan and bake.

So now that you know what you're doing, let's make some muffins!

PART 1
Sweet Escapes

A sweet muffin is a thing of beauty.

From the familiar flavors of crisp apple and buttery walnuts, to the more exotic flavors of saffron and champagne, a sweet muffin will make any morning brighter, any snack time more exciting, and any dessert delightfully different. In this part you'll explore a whole new world of muffins that have a decidedly sweet side.

These sweet muffins may feature a fancy marbled interior or be flavored with creamy mascarpone cheese. Some of them have a surprise filling stuffed right in the middle, while others are studded with bits of tangy fruit, shredded coconut, or everyone's favorite—chocolate! They may have a buttery crumble, a shiny glaze, or they may be perfect just as they are—golden brown and plump from the oven.

So, forget what you think you know about muffins and dive into a world of exotic sweet escapes!

CHAPTER 1

Uniquely Sweet Creations

Muffins need not be boring, and with a few exciting ingredients you can transform the mundane into the mouth-watering. Rather than make the same old standbys, why not venture into exciting new muffin territories? Try a double shot of espresso baked into your morning muffin to jump-start your day. Or think about indulging yourself with a muffin that is filled with an opulent peanut butter cream or even stuffed with a peanut butter cup.

From muffins filled with exotic spices like Middle Eastern *mahlab* and saffron to those that look and taste just like cinnamon rolls, in this chapter the humble sweet muffin gets a glamorous make-over. With the addition of some unusual ingredients and techniques it is easy to make out-of-the-ordinary muffins that have a serious sense of sophistication. So, get out your whisk and break out the muffin pans. It's time to bake some uniquely sweet creations that will take your baking to a whole new level!

Brown Sugar Muffins

Dark brown sugar has a deep molasses flavor that gives these delicious muffins an almost caramel aroma and distinctive taste. Add to that a rich butterscotch glaze, also made with brown sugar and a hint of bourbon, and you have a muffin that is bursting with rich, earthy flavor. Dark brown sugar, which has a higher percentage of residual molasses, will give you the boldest flavor, but you could substitute light brown sugar if you prefer; just add a teaspoon of molasses to the batter to pump up the flavor.

Yields 18 Muffins

2 cups all-purpose flour

1 teaspoon baking powder

½ teaspoon baking soda

½ teaspoon salt

1 cup packed dark brown sugar

¼ cup butter, melted and cooled

1 teaspoon vanilla

1 cup half-and-half

2 eggs

1 recipe Butterscotch Glaze (see Chapter 6)

1. Preheat oven to 350°F and prepare 18 muffin cups with nonstick spray, or line with paper liners.
2. In a large bowl sift together the flour, baking powder, baking soda, and salt. Once sifted, whisk in the dark brown sugar until evenly mixed.
3. In a separate bowl mix together the melted butter, vanilla, half-and-half, and eggs. Whisk until the mixture is well combined.
4. Make a well in the center of the dry ingredients and pour in the wet ingredients. With a wooden spoon or spatula gently fold the mixture until just combined, about 10–12 strokes. Do not overmix.
5. Divide the batter evenly between the prepared muffin cups. Bake for 18–20 minutes, or until the muffins spring back when gently pressed in the center and the tops are golden brown. Cool in the pan for 3 minutes, then remove the muffins from the pan to a wire rack to cool to room temperature.
6. While the muffins are cooling, prepare the Butterscotch Glaze. Dip the tops of the cooled muffins into the warm glaze, allowing the excess to drip off. Place the muffins on a cooling rack and allow the glaze to set, about 1 hour, before serving.

Café Mocha Muffins

Freshly brewed espresso and chocolate make these delicate, chocolate-studded muffins a rival for any coffee-shop creation. For the best flavor, use freshly brewed espresso rather than instant espresso powder. The powder is convenient, but the fresh espresso has an earthy, slightly bitter taste that makes the flavor of the chocolate really pop. Try adding ¼ teaspoon of peppermint extract to these muffins for a festive seasonal touch.

Yields 18 Muffins

1¾ cups all-purpose flour

¼ cup cocoa powder

1 teaspoon baking powder

½ teaspoon baking soda

½ teaspoon salt

½ cup packed light brown sugar

¼ cup sugar

¼ cup butter, melted and cooled

¼ cup canola or vegetable oil

1 teaspoon vanilla

½ cup whole milk

¼ cup freshly brewed espresso, cooled to room temperature

2 eggs

1 cup mini chocolate chips

1 tablespoon all-purpose flour

1. Preheat oven to 350°F and prepare 18 muffin cups with nonstick spray, or line with paper liners.
2. In a large bowl sift together the flour, cocoa powder, baking powder, baking soda, and salt. Once sifted, whisk in the brown sugar and white sugar until evenly mixed.
3. In a separate bowl add the melted butter, oil, vanilla, milk, espresso, and eggs. Whisk until the mixture is well combined.
4. Make a well in the center of the dry ingredients and pour in the wet ingredients. With a wooden spoon or spatula, gently fold the mixture until just combined, about 10 strokes. Do not overmix.
5. In a small bowl combine the chocolate chips with the flour until the chips are coated. Pour the chips into the batter and fold to evenly distribute, about 3 strokes.
6. Divide the batter evenly between the prepared muffin cups. Bake for 18–20 minutes, or until the muffins spring back when gently pressed in the center and the tops are golden brown. Cool in the pan for 3 minutes, then remove the muffins from the pan to cool on a wire rack. Enjoy warm.

Carrot Spice Muffins

Carrot cake's spicy finish and moistness make it extremely popular. This muffin takes these upscale qualities and uses freshly grated carrot, combined with nutty whole-wheat flour and toasty pecans, to create a hearty yet temptingly moist treat. To keep the texture of this muffin as light as possible, be sure to finely grate the carrots. This way the carrot will be evenly distributed throughout the muffin without any chewy chunks.

Yields 18 Muffins

1½ cups all-purpose flour

½ cup whole-wheat flour

¾ teaspoon baking powder

¾ teaspoon baking soda

½ teaspoon salt

½ teaspoon cinnamon

¼ teaspoon nutmeg

¼ teaspoon cardamom

1 cup packed light brown sugar

⅓ cup canola or vegetable oil

1 teaspoon vanilla

¾ cup buttermilk

2 eggs

1 cup finely grated carrot

½ cup finely chopped pecans

1 recipe Cream Cheese Drizzle
(see Chapter 6)

1. Preheat oven to 350°F and prepare 18 muffin cups with nonstick spray, or line with paper liners.
2. In a large bowl sift together the flour, whole-wheat flour, baking powder, baking soda, salt, cinnamon, nutmeg, and cardamom. Once sifted, whisk in the brown sugar until evenly mixed.
3. In a separate bowl add the oil, vanilla, buttermilk, and eggs. Whisk until the mixture is well combined.
4. Make a well in the center of the dry ingredients and pour in the wet ingredients. With a wooden spoon or spatula, gently fold the mixture until just combined, about 10 strokes. Do not overmix. Add the carrots and pecans into the batter and fold to evenly distribute, about 3 strokes.
5. Divide the batter evenly between the prepared muffin cups. Bake for 18–20 minutes, or until the muffins spring back when gently pressed in the center and the tops are golden brown. Cool in the pan for 3 minutes, then remove the muffins from the pan to cool on a wire rack. Enjoy warm.

Cherry Mahlab Muffins

A traditional ingredient in Middle Eastern and Mediterranean sweets, *mahlab* is an exciting ingredient that will have everyone wondering what spice you used! *Mahlab* is the dried seed of the Saint Lucie cherry, and once ground, the seeds have an exotic, slightly bitter flavor. In baked goods this ingredient imparts subtle flavors of cherry and almond, along with a delicate aroma. *Mahlab* is very perishable once ground so it is best to get the whole seeds and grind them as needed.

Yields 18 Muffins

1 cup orange juice

1 cup dried cherries

2 cups all-purpose flour

1 teaspoon baking powder

½ teaspoon baking soda

½ teaspoon salt

1 teaspoon ground *mahlab*

2 teaspoons orange zest

1 cup sugar

⅓ cup butter, melted and cooled

1 teaspoon vanilla

½ cup buttermilk

2 eggs

1 recipe Orange Glaze
(see Chapter 6)

1. Preheat oven to 350°F and prepare 18 muffin cups with nonstick spray, or line with paper liners.
2. In a small pot over medium heat, add the orange juice and dry cherries. Bring the mixture to a boil, then remove the pot from the heat, cover with a lid, and allow to stand for 30 minutes. Strain the cherries and reserve ¼ cup of the juice.
3. In a large bowl sift together the flour, baking powder, baking soda, salt, and *mahlab*. Once sifted, whisk in the orange zest and sugar until evenly mixed.
4. In a separate bowl add the reserved orange-cherry juice, melted butter, vanilla, buttermilk, and eggs. Whisk until the mixture is well combined.
5. Make a well in the center of the dry ingredients and pour in the wet ingredients. With a wooden spoon or spatula, gently fold the mixture until just combined, about 10 strokes. Do not overmix. Add the cherries into the batter and fold to evenly distribute, about 3 strokes.
6. Divide the batter evenly between the prepared muffin cups. Bake for 18–20 minutes, or until the muffins spring back when gently pressed in the center and the tops are golden brown. Cool in the pan for 3 minutes, then remove the muffins from the pan to a wire rack to cool to room temperature.
7. Dip the tops of the muffins into the warm Orange Glaze, allowing the excess to drip off. Place the muffins on a cooling rack and allow the glaze to set, about 1 hour, before serving.

Citrus Cheesecake Muffins

These lemony muffins have a smooth cheesecake center that's made even more irresistible when topped with a buttery brown-sugar topping. In addition, freshly grated lemon zest gives these muffins a refreshing burst of flavor and a fresh lemony scent. The zest contains all the essential oils of the citrus so it provides a very concentrated lemon flavor. You could substitute orange or lime zest if you wanted, or combine all three for a more unique taste.

Yields 12 Muffins

6 ounces cream cheese, at room temperature

⅓ cup powdered sugar

1 tablespoon fresh lemon juice

1 egg

2 cups all-purpose flour

1½ teaspoons baking powder

½ teaspoon salt

¾ cup sugar

½ cup butter, melted and cooled

1 tablespoon freshly grated lemon zest

½ teaspoon vanilla extract

1 egg

1 cup buttermilk

1 recipe Brown Sugar Streusel (see Chapter 6)

1. Preheat oven to 350°F and line a 12-cup muffin pan with paper liners.
2. In a medium bowl beat together the cream cheese, powdered sugar, lemon juice, and egg until smooth and creamy. Set aside.
3. In a large bowl whisk together the flour, baking powder, salt, and sugar until evenly combined.
4. In a medium bowl whisk together the butter, lemon zest, vanilla, egg, and buttermilk until well mixed.
5. Make a well in the center of the dry ingredients and pour in the wet ingredients. With a wooden spoon or spatula, gently fold the mixture until just combined, about 12 strokes. Do not overmix.
6. Divide the muffin batter evenly between the prepared muffin cups. Drop a tablespoon of the cream cheese mixture into the center of each muffin cup, then top with the Brown Sugar Streusel.
7. Bake for 20–25 minutes, or until the streusel is browned and the muffins spring back when gently pressed near the edge. Cool in the pan for 5 minutes, then remove from the pan and cool on a wire rack. Enjoy warm or at room temperature.

Citrus Cheesecake Muffins with Brown Sugar Streusel (see Chapter 6)

Chocolate Chip Overload Muffins

With not one, not two, but three kinds of chocolate chips, these moist, chocolaty muffins are most certainly for chocolate lovers. And, as if the variety of chips isn't enough, these muffins have two total cups of chips, which makes them absolutely packed with chocolaty goodness. The ratio of semisweet chips to the white chocolate and milk chocolate chips is 2 to 1, but feel free to play with the ratio to suit your personal chocolate preference. Peanut butter chips are also a good option here, if you are so inclined.

Yields 18 Muffins

1¾ cups all-purpose flour

¼ cup cocoa powder

¾ teaspoon baking powder

¾ teaspoon baking soda

½ teaspoon salt

1 cup packed light brown sugar

⅓ cup canola or vegetable oil

1 teaspoon vanilla

¾ cup milk

2 eggs

1 cup semisweet chocolate chips

½ cup white chocolate chips

½ cup milk chocolate chips

1 tablespoon all-purpose flour

1. Preheat oven to 350°F and prepare 18 muffin cups with nonstick spray, or line with paper liners.
2. In a large bowl sift together the flour, cocoa powder, baking powder, baking soda, and salt. Once sifted, whisk in the brown sugar until evenly mixed.
3. In a separate bowl add the oil, vanilla, milk, and eggs. Whisk until the mixture is well combined.
4. Make a well in the center of the dry ingredients and pour in the wet ingredients. With a wooden spoon or spatula, gently fold the mixture until just combined, about 10 strokes. Do not overmix. In a small bowl combine all the chocolate chips with the flour until the chips are coated. Pour the chips into the batter and fold to evenly distribute, about 3 strokes.
5. Divide the batter evenly between the prepared muffin cups. Bake for 18–20 minutes, or until the muffins spring back when gently pressed in the center and the tops are golden brown. Cool in the pan for 3 minutes, then remove the muffins from the pan to cool on a wire rack. Enjoy warm.

Cinnamon Apple Corn Muffins

These corn muffins are light, tender, and flavored with aromatic honey and bits of tart Granny Smith apple. Serve these for breakfast with a little honey butter or some sweetened cream cheese, or shake things up and serve them as an unexpected side dish to lunch or dinner. These muffins pair particularly well with grilled meat and barbecue because their slight sweetness helps cleanse the palate.

Yields 12 Muffins

¾ cup cornmeal

1 cup all-purpose flour

3 tablespoons white sugar

1½ teaspoons baking powder

½ teaspoon salt

½ teaspoon cinnamon

1 egg

¼ cup honey

¼ cup butter, melted and cooled

1 cup buttermilk

1 Granny Smith apple, peeled, cored, and chopped

Salted Caramel Butter, optional (see Chapter 5)

1. Preheat oven to 350°F and either spray a 12-cup muffin pan with nonstick spray or line with paper liners.
2. In a large bowl whisk together the cornmeal, flour, sugar, baking powder, salt, and cinnamon until well mixed.
3. In a medium bowl add the egg, honey, butter, and buttermilk, and whisk until evenly combined.
4. Make a well in the center of the dry ingredients and pour in the wet ingredients. With a wooden spoon or spatula, gently fold the mixture until just combined, about 10 strokes. Do not overmix. Pour the apple into the batter and fold to evenly distribute, about 3 strokes.
5. Divide the batter evenly between the prepared muffin cups. Bake for 18–20 minutes, or until the muffins spring back when gently pressed in the center and the tops are golden brown. Cool in the pan for 3 minutes, then remove the muffins from the pan to cool on a wire rack. Enjoy these muffins warm with Salted Caramel Butter, if desired.

Cinnamon Roll Muffins

Cinnamon rolls are the ultimate comfort food, but they take a while to make properly. In contrast, this muffin takes a fraction of the time to make, yet provides all the comforting flavor of its yeasty counterpart. Rather than make a yeast dough, or even a traditional muffin batter, this recipe uses a modified biscuit dough to make tender, buttery, satisfyingly moist cinnamon rolls that you can have from idea to first bite in less than an hour. And because they are baked individually they freeze well for those times when you need some cinnamon-scented comfort!

Yields 16 Muffins

¼ cup packed light brown sugar

4 cups all-purpose flour

2 teaspoons baking powder

1 teaspoon baking soda

½ teaspoon salt

¾ cup solid butter, divided use

1 cup sour cream, at room temperature

½ cup whole milk, at room temperature

1 cup packed light brown sugar

2 teaspoons cinnamon

½ cup butter, melted and cooled

2 ounces cream cheese, at room temperature

2 tablespoons butter, at room temperature

1 teaspoon vanilla

1 cup powdered sugar

1. Preheat oven to 350°F and prepare 16 muffin cups with nonstick spray.

2. In a medium bowl add the brown sugar, flour, baking powder, baking soda, and salt. Whisk to combine. Dice ¼ cup of the solid butter into small cubes and rub it into the flour mixture until it looks like coarse sand. Set aside.

3. Melt the remaining ½ cup solid butter and in a separate bowl, combine it with the sour cream and milk. Pour the mixture over the flour and stir until just combined, about 5–8 strokes. Lightly flour a work surface and turn out the dough. Press it into a rough square that is ¼-inch thick.

4. In a small bowl combine the brown sugar, cinnamon, and ½ cup melted butter until they form a smooth paste. Spread the filling evenly over the dough. Carefully roll the dough into a log, then slice into 1-inch rolls.

5. Place the rolls into the prepared pan and bake for 20–25 minutes, or until the rolls are golden brown on the top and puffed. Cool for 5 minutes in the pan, then turn the rolls out onto a wire rack.

6. Whisk together the cream cheese, 2 tablespoons room-temperature butter, and vanilla until smooth. Slowly add in the powdered sugar until the frosting is at your preferred thickness. You may add more powdered sugar if you like the frosting stiffer. Spread the frosting over the warm rolls, allowing some to drip down the sides. Serve warm.

Cornmeal Buttermilk Muffins

Stone-ground cornmeal has a coarser texture than regular, commercially produced cornmeal. Because stone-ground cornmeal is coarsely ground it keeps some of the hull and germ, which adds a more interesting flavor to whatever dish it is baked in. In these muffins the stone-ground cornmeal is used along with bacon drippings in place of oil or butter. The drippings add a subtle bacon flavor and extra richness that your family and friends will savor.

Yields 12 Muffins

1 cup stone-ground cornmeal

1¼ cups all-purpose flour

1½ teaspoons baking powder

¼ teaspoon baking soda

½ teaspoon salt

1 egg

2 tablespoons honey

⅓ cup bacon drippings

1 cup buttermilk

Whipped Honey Lavender Butter, optional (see Chapter 5)

1. Preheat oven to 350°F and either spray a 12-cup muffin pan with nonstick spray or line with paper liners.
2. In a large bowl whisk together the cornmeal, flour, baking powder, baking soda, and salt until well combined.
3. In a medium bowl add the egg, honey, bacon drippings, and buttermilk. Whisk until evenly mixed.
4. Make a well in the center of the dry ingredients and pour in the wet ingredients. With a wooden spoon or spatula, gently fold the mixture until just combined, about 10–12 strokes. Do not overmix.
5. Divide the batter evenly between the prepared muffin cups. Bake for 18–20 minutes, or until the muffins spring back when gently pressed in the center and the tops are golden brown. Cool in the pan for 3 minutes, then remove the muffins from the pan to a wire rack to cool. Enjoy warm with Whipped Honey Lavender Butter, if desired.

Coconut and Lime Muffins

Coconut milk, the creamy liquid pressed from the flesh of fresh coconut, is used in this recipe instead of milk to add both richness and extra coconut flavor. Coconut milk can usually be found in the Asian section of most grocery stores. To bake the best possible muffin, use full-fat coconut milk. Light coconut milk has less fat than regular coconut milk, but it also has less flavor. Substituting light for regular will result in muffins that are not as moist, flavorful, or gourmet.

Yields 18 Muffins

2 cups all-purpose flour

1 teaspoon baking powder

½ teaspoon baking soda

½ teaspoon salt

1 cup sugar

⅓ cup canola or vegetable oil

1 teaspoon vanilla

1 tablespoon freshly grated lime zest

1 tablespoon fresh lime juice

¾ cup coconut milk

2 eggs

1½ cups shredded coconut

1 recipe Coconut Glaze (see Chapter 6)

1. Preheat oven to 350°F and prepare 18 muffin cups with nonstick spray, or line with paper liners.
2. In a large bowl sift together the flour, baking powder, baking soda, and salt. Once sifted, whisk in the sugar until evenly mixed.
3. In a separate bowl add the oil, vanilla, lime zest, lime juice, coconut milk, and eggs. Whisk until the mixture is well combined.
4. Make a well in the center of the dry ingredients and pour in the wet ingredients. With a wooden spoon or spatula, gently fold the mixture until just combined, about 10 strokes. Do not overmix. Add 1 cup of the shredded coconut and mix until combined, about 3 strokes.
5. Divide the batter evenly between the prepared muffin cups. Bake for 18–20 minutes, or until the muffins spring back when gently pressed in the center and the tops are golden brown. Cool in the pan for 3 minutes, then remove the muffins from the pan to a wire rack to cool to room temperature.
6. Once the muffins have cooled, prepare the Coconut Glaze. Dip the tops of the muffins into the warm glaze, allowing the excess to drip off. Place the muffins on a cooling rack and, while the glaze is still wet, sprinkle the remaining ½ cup shredded coconut over the tops. Allow the glaze to set, about 1 hour, before serving.

Coconut and Lime Muffins with Coconut Glaze (see Chapter 6)

Dark Chocolate Orange Zest Muffins

Fresh orange zest gives these intense chocolate muffins a bright, fresh flavor that keeps them from being too rich and also adds a huge aromatic impact. You'll smell a rich chocolate aroma, but just underneath it you'll be able to discern the almost sunny scent of orange. And, as if these muffins weren't amazing enough, they also freeze very well, so a little chocolate orange therapy is never too far away!

Yields 12 Muffins

1¾ cups all-purpose flour

2 teaspoons baking powder

½ teaspoon baking soda

3 tablespoons Dutch-processed cocoa powder

¼ teaspoon salt

¾ cup packed light brown sugar

1 cup buttermilk

⅓ cup vegetable oil

1 egg

1 tablespoon freshly grated orange zest

1 teaspoon vanilla

1 cup semisweet chocolate chips

1. Preheat oven to 350°F and either spray a 12-cup muffin pan with nonstick spray or line with paper liners.
2. In a large bowl sift together the flour, baking powder, baking soda, cocoa powder, salt, and brown sugar.
3. In a medium bowl combine the buttermilk, oil, egg, orange zest, and vanilla. Whisk until smooth.
4. Make a well in the center of the dry ingredients and pour in the wet ingredients. With a wooden spoon or spatula, gently fold the mixture until just combined, about 10 strokes. Do not overmix. Add ¾ cup of the chocolate chips and fold to mix, about 2–3 strokes.
5. Divide the batter evenly between the prepared muffin cups, then dot the tops with the remaining chocolate chips. Bake for 18–20 minutes, or until the muffins spring back when gently pressed in the center. Cool in the pan for 3 minutes, then remove the muffins from the pan to a wire rack to cool. Enjoy warm.

Double Shot Espresso Muffins

Looking to add a little extra buzz to your mornings? You could have another cup of coffee, but why not change things up and get your caffeine fix in muffin form? These muffins are pure coffee goodness, topped with a mocha glaze, so you get all the flavors of fresh-brewed espresso without visiting the local barista! If you want to add a little chocolate, try adding ½ cup mini chocolate chips to the batter.

Yields 18 Muffins

2 cups all-purpose flour

1½ teaspoons baking powder

½ teaspoon baking soda

½ teaspoon salt

¼ teaspoon cinnamon

1 cup sugar

⅓ cup vegetable or canola oil

1 teaspoon vanilla

½ cup whole milk

¼ cup fresh-brewed espresso, cooled

2 eggs

1 recipe Mocha Glaze (see Chapter 6)

1. Preheat oven to 350°F and prepare 18 muffin cups with nonstick spray, or line with paper liners.
2. In a large bowl sift together the flour, baking powder, baking soda, salt, and cinnamon. Once sifted, whisk in the sugar until evenly mixed.
3. In a separate bowl add the oil, vanilla, milk, espresso, and eggs. Whisk until the mixture is well combined.
4. Make a well in the center of the dry ingredients and pour in the wet ingredients. With a wooden spoon or spatula, gently fold the mixture until just combined, about 10–12 strokes. Do not overmix.
5. Divide the batter evenly between the prepared muffin cups. Bake for 18–20 minutes, or until the muffins spring back when gently pressed in the center and the tops are golden brown. Cool in the pan for 3 minutes, then remove the muffins from the pan to a wire rack to cool to room temperature.
6. Once the muffins have cooled, prepare the Mocha Glaze. Dip the tops of the muffins into the warm glaze, allowing the excess to drip off. Place the muffins on a cooling rack and allow the glaze to set, about 1 hour, before serving.

Jam-Filled Peanut Butter Muffins

These muffins are a fresh take on the classic lunchbox combination, peanut butter and jelly. Peanut butter not only flavors these unique muffins but also makes them incredibly moist and tender. On the outside these peanut butter muffins may appear to be just average, but when you bite into the center you'll find a little pocket of jelly goodness. It takes one bite to reveal the surprise and, combined with the peanut butter muffin, it is utterly divine. These muffins truly are a sophisticated version of a classic that is guaranteed to bring out the kid in everyone.

Yields 18 Muffins

2 cups all-purpose flour

½ cup sugar

¼ cup packed light brown sugar

1 teaspoon baking powder

½ teaspoon baking soda

½ teaspoon salt

¼ cup butter, melted and cooled

½ cup peanut butter, melted and cooled

1 teaspoon vanilla

¾ cup buttermilk

¼ cup sour cream

2 eggs

¾ cup grape or strawberry jam

1 recipe Peanut Butter Drizzle (see Chapter 6)

1. Preheat oven to 350°F and prepare 18 muffin cups with nonstick spray, or line with paper liners.
2. In a large bowl sift together the flour, sugar, brown sugar, baking powder, baking soda, and salt.
3. In a separate bowl add the butter, peanut butter, vanilla, buttermilk, sour cream, and eggs. Whisk until the mixture is well combined.
4. Make a well in the center of the dry ingredients and pour in the wet ingredients. With a wooden spoon or spatula, gently fold the mixture until just combined, about 10–12 strokes. Do not overmix.
5. Divide the batter evenly between the prepared muffin cups. Bake for 18–20 minutes, or until the muffins spring back when gently pressed in the center and the tops are golden brown. Cool in the pan for 3 minutes, then remove the muffins from the pan to a wire rack to cool to room temperature.
6. Once the muffins are cooled completely, poke a small paring knife into the center of each muffin in a cross pattern about 1-inch deep. Take a pastry bag fitted with a small star tip and fill it with the jam. Press the tip into the cross and pipe in about 1 tablespoon of jam. Clean any excess jam off the tops of the muffins before decorating the tops with the Peanut Butter Drizzle.

Lemon Poppy Seed Muffins

A good lemon poppy seed muffin needs to taste like two things: fresh lemon and poppy seeds. The tangy, light lemony burst that refreshes your palate is due to three sources: zest, juice, and a glaze made of limoncello, an Italian lemon liqueur. Combined with the earthy flavor of black poppy seeds, this tempting muffin is as pretty to look at as it is delightful to eat!

Yields 18 Muffins

2 cups all-purpose flour

2 teaspoons baking powder

½ teaspoon baking soda

¼ teaspoon salt

¾ cup sugar

1 cup buttermilk

⅓ cup vegetable oil

2 eggs

1 tablespoon freshly grated lemon zest

1 tablespoon fresh lemon juice

1 teaspoon vanilla

¼ cup poppy seeds

1 recipe Limoncello Glaze (see Chapter 6)

1. Preheat oven to 350°F and prepare 18 muffin cups with nonstick spray, or line with paper liners.
2. In a large bowl sift together the flour, baking powder, baking soda, salt, and sugar.
3. In a medium bowl combine the buttermilk, oil, egg, lemon zest, lemon juice, and vanilla. Whisk until smooth.
4. Make a well in the center of the dry ingredients and pour in the wet ingredients. With a wooden spoon or spatula, gently fold the mixture until just combined, about 10 strokes. Do not overmix. Add the poppy seeds and fold to mix, about 2–3 strokes.
5. Divide the batter evenly between the prepared muffin cups. Bake for 18–20 minutes, or until the muffins spring back when gently pressed in the center. Cool in the pan for 3 minutes, then remove the muffins from the pan to a wire rack to cool completely.
6. Once the muffins have cooled, prepare the Limoncello Glaze. Dip the tops of the muffins into the warm glaze, allowing the excess to drip off. Place the muffins on a cooling rack and allow the glaze to set, about 1 hour, before serving.

Malted Chocolate Muffins

Malted milk powder has a particular flavor most associated with soda-shop treats and, in fact, this muffin was inspired by the chocolate malt. These muffins are not terribly chocolaty—there are only 2 tablespoons of cocoa powder in this recipe. Instead, the cocoa is a subtle backdrop that the malty flavor then plays off. Be sure to use plain malted milk powder when making these muffins. Some brands add chocolate or vanilla flavoring to malted milk powder, which can dilute the malted taste.

Yields 18 Muffins

1¾ cups all-purpose flour

1½ teaspoons baking powder

½ teaspoon baking soda

½ teaspoon salt

2 tablespoons cocoa powder

1 cup packed light brown sugar

¼ cup malted milk powder

⅓ cup butter, melted and cooled

1 teaspoon vanilla

1 cup half-and-half

2 eggs

1. Preheat oven to 350°F and prepare 18 muffin cups with nonstick spray, or line with paper liners.
2. In a large bowl sift together the flour, baking powder, baking soda, salt, and cocoa powder. Once sifted, whisk in the brown sugar and malted milk powder until evenly mixed.
3. In a separate bowl add the melted butter, vanilla, half-and-half, and eggs. Whisk until the mixture is well combined.
4. Make a well in the center of the dry ingredients and pour in the wet ingredients. With a wooden spoon or spatula, gently fold the mixture until just combined, about 10–12 strokes. Do not overmix.
5. Divide the batter evenly between the prepared muffin cups. Bake for 18–20 minutes, or until the muffins spring back when gently pressed in the center and the tops look dry. Cool in the pan for 3 minutes, then remove the muffins from the pan to a wire rack to cool. Enjoy slightly warm or at room temperature.

Mascarpone Pound Cake Muffins

Similar to cream cheese, mascarpone cheese is a smooth creamy Italian cheese that has a mild, yet very rich flavor. But in this recipe the mascarpone is used both for flavor and to add a creamy texture to the crumb of this muffin. These sophisticated muffins are like individual pound cakes, and when paired with fresh berries and whipped cream they make an excellent dessert.

Yields 12 Muffins

½ cup butter, softened

1 cup sugar

2 eggs

½ cup mascarpone cheese

1 teaspoon vanilla-bean paste

1 teaspoon lemon zest

1¾ cups all-purpose flour

½ teaspoon salt

½ teaspoon baking soda

1 recipe Vanilla Bean Icing (see Chapter 6)

1. Preheat oven to 350°F and either spray a 12-cup muffin pan with nonstick spray or line with paper liners.
2. In a large bowl cream together the butter and sugar until very light and fluffy, about 10 minutes. Add eggs, one at a time, beating 3 minutes after each addition. Add the mascarpone cheese, vanilla-bean paste, and lemon zest, and beat for 5 minutes.
3. In a separate bowl sift together the flour, salt, and baking soda. Pour the dry ingredients over the wet and gently mix until just moistened.
4. Divide the batter among the prepared muffin cups. Bake for 18–20 minutes, or until the muffins are golden brown and the cake springs back when gently pressed in the center. Cool for 5 minutes before removing from pan to a wire rack to cool completely.
5. Once the muffins are cooled, drizzle Vanilla Bean Icing over the muffins. Allow the icing to set for 1 hour before serving.

Dulce de Leche Muffins with Cinnamon Pecan Streusel (see Chapter 6)

Dulce de Leche Muffins

Dulce de leche is a popular Latin American ingredient made from sweetened condensed milk that is slowly cooked until the sugars caramelize and the milk becomes sticky and thick. The flavor is like a very rich caramel and it is just lovely when spread on cakes or stirred into coffee. Here the dulce de leche is swirled into these decadent muffins and topped with a cinnamon pecan topping.

Yields 18 Muffins

2¼ cups all-purpose flour

1 teaspoon baking powder

½ teaspoon baking soda

½ teaspoon salt

1 cup sugar

⅓ cup butter, melted and cooled

1 teaspoon vanilla

⅔ cup whole milk

2 eggs

⅓ cup dulce de leche

1 recipe Cinnamon Pecan Streusel (see Chapter 6)

1. Preheat oven to 350°F and prepare 18 muffin cups with nonstick spray, or line with paper liners.
2. In a large bowl sift together the flour, baking powder, baking soda, and salt. Once sifted, whisk in the sugar until evenly mixed.
3. In a separate bowl add the melted butter, vanilla, milk, and eggs. Whisk until the mixture is well combined.
4. Make a well in the center of the dry ingredients and pour in the wet ingredients. With a wooden spoon or spatula, gently fold the mixture until just combined, about 10–12 strokes. Do not overmix.
5. In a microwave-safe bowl heat the dulce de leche until it is softened, about 30 seconds. Scoop ⅓ cup of the muffin batter into the dulce de leche and whisk until smooth.
6. Divide half the batter evenly between the prepared muffin cups. Spoon the dulce de leche mixture over the batter, then top with the remaining muffin batter. With a toothpick or thin knife, make a figure-eight pattern in the muffin. Top the muffins with the Cinnamon Pecan Streusel.
7. Bake for 18–20 minutes, or until the muffins spring back when gently pressed in the center and the tops are golden brown. Cool in the pan for 3 minutes, then remove the muffins from the pan to a wire rack to cool. Enjoy slightly warm or at room temperature.

Peanut Butter Butterscotch Crumb Muffins

If you love peanut butter, these muffins are for you! The muffin itself is flavored with peanut butter, but studded in the muffin batter are little nuggets of joy in the form of peanut butter chips. And as if that isn't amazing enough, the muffins are topped with a butterscotch crumble, which helps bring out the nuttiness of the peanut butter. If you wanted to add an extra layer of deliciousness to this muffin, substitute chunky peanut butter for the smooth version called for in the recipe to add texture and more peanut impact.

Yields 18 Muffins

2 cups all-purpose flour

¾ cup packed light brown sugar

1½ teaspoons baking powder

½ teaspoon baking soda

½ teaspoon salt

¼ cup butter, melted and cooled

½ cup smooth peanut butter, melted and cooled

1 teaspoon vanilla

1 cup buttermilk

2 eggs

1 cup peanut butter chips

1 recipe Butterscotch Crumble (see Chapter 6)

1. Preheat oven to 350°F and prepare 18 muffin cups with nonstick spray, or line with paper liners.
2. In a large bowl sift together the flour, brown sugar, baking powder, baking soda, and salt.
3. In a separate bowl add the butter, peanut butter, vanilla, buttermilk, and eggs. Whisk until the mixture is well combined.
4. Make a well in the center of the dry ingredients and pour in the wet ingredients. With a wooden spoon or spatula, gently fold the mixture until just combined, about 10 strokes. Do not overmix. Add the peanut butter chips and fold to mix, about 2–3 strokes.
5. Divide the batter evenly between the prepared muffin cups. Top each muffin with the Butterscotch Crumble and bake for 18–20 minutes, or until the muffins spring back when gently pressed in the center and the tops are golden brown. Cool in the pan for 3 minutes, then remove the muffins from the pan to a wire rack to cool to room temperature.

Peanut Butter Cream–Filled Banana Muffins

Say goodbye to plain old banana muffins! Hidden in the center of these moist banana muffins is a creamy peanut butter surprise. Peanut butter and banana are a favorite combination, but here they are used in a less obvious, more gourmet way. In this recipe, the peanut butter filling is not overpowering; instead, the flavor acts as a nice contrast to the banana, making this the perfect snack for any peanut butter–banana craving!

Yields 12 Muffins

2 medium ripe bananas, mashed (about 1 cup)

½ cup buttermilk

¼ cup butter, melted and cooled

1 egg

1 teaspoon vanilla

1 cup all-purpose flour

¾ cup sugar

¼ teaspoon cinnamon

½ teaspoon baking soda

¼ teaspoon baking powder

⅛ teaspoon salt

1 teaspoon boiling water

3½ ounces marshmallow fluff

¼ cup vegetable shortening

3 tablespoons powdered sugar

2 tablespoons peanut butter

½ teaspoon vanilla

Peanut Butter Drizzle (see Chapter 6)

¼ cup crushed roasted peanuts

1. Preheat oven to 350°F and either spray a 12-cup muffin pan with nonstick spray or line with paper liners.
2. In a medium bowl whisk together the banana, buttermilk, butter, egg, and vanilla. Set aside.
3. In a large bowl add the flour, sugar, cinnamon, baking soda, baking powder, and salt. Whisk until well combined. Make a well in the center of the dry ingredients and pour in the wet ingredients. With a wooden spoon or spatula, gently fold the mixture until just combined, about 10–12 strokes. Do not overmix.
4. Divide the batter evenly between the prepared muffin cups and bake for 18–20 minutes, or until the muffins spring back when gently pressed in the center and the tops are golden brown. Cool in the pan for 3 minutes, then remove the muffins from the pan to a wire rack to cool to room temperature.
5. While the muffins bake, prepare the filling. In a medium bowl combine the water, marshmallow fluff, shortening, powdered sugar, peanut butter, and vanilla. Beat until smooth, then load the mixture into a piping bag fitted with a star tip.
6. Once the muffins are cooled completely, poke a small paring knife into the center of each muffin in a cross pattern about 1-inch deep. Take the pastry bag filled with the marshmallow fluff mixture and press the tip into the cross, and pipe in about 1 tablespoon. Clean the excess fluff off the tops of the muffins before decorating them with the Peanut Butter Drizzle and crushed peanuts.

Peppermint White Chocolate Muffins

Peppermint and white chocolate play very well together and you'll often find them paired up in coffee shops and in candy. Mint can overwhelm the delicate flavor of white chocolate so this recipe uses a lightly flavored muffin that is given a little mint boost with a minty glaze. If you can find them, white chocolate chunks are lovely in place of white chocolate chips. The chunks provide slightly larger nuggets of white chocolate love.

Yields 18 Muffins

2 cups all-purpose flour

1¼ teaspoons baking powder

½ teaspoon baking soda

½ teaspoon salt

1 cup sugar

⅓ cup butter, melted and cooled

1 teaspoon vanilla

¼ teaspoon mint extract

1 cup whole milk

2 eggs

1 cup white chocolate chips

1 tablespoon flour

1 recipe Minty Glaze (see Chapter 6)

1. Preheat oven to 350°F and prepare 18 muffin cups with nonstick spray, or line with paper liners.
2. In a large bowl sift together the flour, baking powder, baking soda, and salt. Once sifted, whisk in the sugar until evenly mixed.
3. In a separate bowl add the melted butter, vanilla, mint extract, milk, and eggs. Whisk until the mixture is well combined.
4. Make a well in the center of the dry ingredients and pour in the wet ingredients. With a wooden spoon or spatula, gently fold the mixture until just combined, about 10 strokes. Do not overmix. In a small bowl combine the white chocolate chips with the flour and toss to coat. Add the coated chips to the batter and fold to combine, about 2–3 strokes.
5. Divide the batter evenly between the prepared muffin cups. Bake for 18–20 minutes, or until the muffins spring back when gently pressed in the center and the tops are golden brown. Cool in the pan for 3 minutes, then remove the muffins from the pan to a wire rack to cool to room temperature.
6. Once the muffins have cooled, prepare the Minty Glaze. Dip the muffin tops into the warm glaze, allowing the excess to drip off. Place the muffins on a cooling rack and allow the glaze to set, about 1 hour, before serving.

Pistachio Rose Water Muffins

Rose water and pistachio are a popular flavor combination in Persian cooking. While their inclusion may seem very exotic, the flavors pair exceptionally well together in sweet recipes such as baklava and cookies. In this recipe the rose water gives the muffins a deep floral aroma and a subtle rose flavor that balances the almost sharp flavor of the pistachios. Rose water (also known as rose syrup) may be difficult to find, but you can order it online or find it in specialty shops. If there is added sugar in the brand that you buy, be sure to reduce the sugar by at least ¼ cup to avoid making the muffins too sweet.

Yields 18 Muffins

2 cups all-purpose flour

1 teaspoon baking powder

½ teaspoon baking soda

½ teaspoon salt

1 cup sugar

¼ cup canola or vegetable oil

1 teaspoon vanilla

2 tablespoons rose water

1 cup half-and-half

2 eggs

1 cup chopped pistachios

1. Preheat oven to 350°F and prepare 18 muffin cups with nonstick spray, or line with paper liners.
2. In a large bowl sift together the flour, baking powder, baking soda, and salt. Once sifted, whisk in the sugar until evenly mixed.
3. In a separate bowl add the oil, vanilla, rose water, half-and-half, and eggs. Whisk until the mixture is well combined.
4. Make a well in the center of the dry ingredients and pour in the wet ingredients. With a wooden spoon or spatula, gently fold the mixture until just combined, about 10 strokes. Do not overmix. Add the chopped pistachios and mix until combined, about 3 strokes.
5. Divide the batter evenly between the prepared muffin cups. Bake for 18–20 minutes, or until the muffins spring back when gently pressed in the center and the tops are golden brown. Cool in the pan for 3 minutes, then remove the muffins from the pan to a wire rack to cool to room temperature.

Port Poached Pear Muffins

The surprising addition of tender poached pears takes these glam muffins over the top. Usually poached pears are served just as they are, with a scoop of ice cream. Here they are folded into a vanilla batter that is flavored with the sweet poaching liquid. Sweet port wine, luscious pears, and fresh vanilla bean make these muffins a perfect end to a meal—or an exciting way to celebrate any of your day's little achievements!

Yields 18 Muffins

2 Bosc pears, peeled, quartered, and cores removed

2 cups ruby port wine

1 cup water

1 cup sugar

1 cinnamon stick

½ vanilla bean, split and seeds scraped out

2¼ cups all-purpose flour

1 teaspoon baking powder

½ teaspoon baking soda

½ teaspoon salt

1 cup sugar

¼ cup vegetable or canola oil

1 teaspoon vanilla

½ cup half-and-half

2 eggs

1 recipe Brown Sugar Streusel (see Chapter 6)

1. In a medium saucepan combine the pears, port wine, water, sugar, cinnamon stick, and vanilla bean. Heat over medium heat until the sugar dissolves and the mixture just comes to a boil, then reduce the heat to medium low and cook, covered, until the pears are tender, about 15–20 minutes. Remove the pears from the liquid and cool to room temperature, then dice them. Reserve ¼ cup of the poaching liquid.

2. Preheat oven to 350°F and prepare 18 muffin cups with nonstick spray, or line with paper liners.

3. In a large bowl sift together the flour, baking powder, baking soda, and salt. Once sifted, whisk in the sugar until evenly mixed.

4. In a separate bowl add the reserved poaching liquid, oil, vanilla, half-and-half, and eggs. Whisk until the mixture is well combined.

5. Make a well in the center of the dry ingredients and pour in the wet ingredients. With a wooden spoon or spatula, gently fold the mixture until just combined, about 10 strokes. Do not overmix. Add the diced pears and fold to incorporate, about 3 strokes.

6. Divide the batter evenly between the prepared muffin cups and top with the Brown Sugar Streusel. Bake for 18–20 minutes, or until the muffins spring back when gently pressed in the center and the tops are golden brown. Cool in the pan for 3 minutes, then remove the muffins from the pan to a wire rack to cool to room temperature.

Pumpkin Caramel Muffins

When the weather turns brisk there is nothing more welcome—or comforting—than a freshly baked muffin made with warm, rich flavors. Here sweet pumpkin is mixed into a spicy muffin that is glazed with buttery, yet slightly salty caramel. The pumpkin purée mixed into the batter makes this muffin incredibly moist, and the caramel glaze gives the traditional pumpkin muffin a uniquely upscale, modern twist. For a fun finish serve these muffins with some Cinnamon Walnut Cream Cheese Spread (see Chapter 5)!

Yields 18 Muffins

1½ cups sugar

½ cup vegetable oil

2 eggs, lightly beaten

1 cup pumpkin purée

1¾ cups all-purpose flour

1 teaspoon salt

1 teaspoon baking soda

½ teaspoon baking powder

½ teaspoon nutmeg

½ teaspoon allspice

½ teaspoon cinnamon

¼ teaspoon cloves

⅛ teaspoon cardamom

⅔ cup whole milk

1 recipe Salted Caramel Glaze (see Chapter 6)

1. Preheat oven to 350°F and prepare 18 muffin cups with nonstick spray, or line with paper liners.
2. In a large bowl combine the sugar and oil. Add the eggs one at a time until they are completely mixed, then stir in the pumpkin. Set aside.
3. In a separate bowl sift together the flour, salt, baking soda, baking powder, nutmeg, allspice, cinnamon, cloves, and cardamom.
4. Add the flour mixture alternately with the milk to the pumpkin mixture, beginning and ending with the flour.
5. Divide the batter evenly between the prepared muffin cups. Bake for 18–20 minutes, or until the muffins spring back when gently pressed in the center and the tops are golden brown. Cool in the pan for 3 minutes, then remove the muffins from the pan to a wire rack to cool to room temperature.
6. Once the muffins have cooled, prepare the Salted Caramel Glaze. Drizzle the caramel over the tops of the muffins. Place the muffins on a cooling rack and allow the glaze to set, about 1 hour, before serving.

Chocolate Strawberry Marble Muffins

Chocolate Strawberry Marble Muffins

Gentle swirls of rosy strawberry and decadent chocolate make this muffin very unique. With flavors similar to chocolate-dipped strawberries—a romantic favorite—this muffin is a sweet, pretty little nibble that is sure to impress. This recipe does call for a little red food coloring to enhance the berry color of the strawberry and to help define the colors in the swirl, but it is not required.

Yields 18 Muffins

2 cups all-purpose flour

1 teaspoon baking powder

½ teaspoon baking soda

½ teaspoon salt

1 cup sugar

½ cup butter, melted and cooled

1 teaspoon vanilla

¾ cup half-and-half

2 eggs

¼ cup melted chocolate

¼ cup strawberry jam

3 drops red food coloring

3 tablespoons semisweet chocolate chips, melted

1. Preheat oven to 350°F and prepare 18 muffin cups with nonstick spray, or line with paper liners.
2. In a large bowl sift together the flour, baking powder, baking soda, and salt. Once sifted, whisk in the sugar until evenly mixed.
3. In a separate bowl add the melted butter, vanilla, half-and-half, and eggs. Whisk until the mixture is well combined.
4. Make a well in the center of the dry ingredients and pour in the wet ingredients. With a wooden spoon or spatula, gently fold the mixture until just combined, about 10 strokes. Do not overmix.
5. Divide the batter into two bowls. Into one add the melted chocolate, into the other add the strawberry jam and food coloring. Mix both until they are evenly combined, about 5 strokes each.
6. Spoon the batters into the prepared muffin cups, layering the chocolate and strawberry batters evenly. With a butter knife make a figure-eight pattern in each muffin one time. Bake for 18–20 minutes, or until the muffins spring back when gently pressed in the center and the tops are golden brown. Cool in the pan for 3 minutes, then remove the muffins from the pan to a wire rack to cool to room temperature. Once cooled drizzle the tops of the muffins with the melted chocolate.

Rocky Road Streusel Muffins

Rocky road is a popular dessert flavor the world over, and here the nuts, marshmallows, and chocolate are baked into a tender muffin. To give this muffin a bit of an edge, the almonds in this recipe are roasted and salted. This gives the muffins an even deeper flavor, and the salt helps balance the sweetness of the marshmallows and chocolate chips. If you want to make these muffins even more amazing, drizzle them with a chocolate glaze and sprinkle the tops with chopped almonds.

Yields 18 Muffins

1¾ cups all-purpose flour

¼ cup Dutch-processed cocoa powder

1¼ teaspoons baking powder

½ teaspoon baking soda

½ teaspoon salt

1 cup packed light brown sugar

⅓ cup butter, melted and cooled

1 teaspoon vanilla

¾ cup half-and-half

2 eggs

¾ cup semisweet chocolate chips

¾ cup mini marshmallows

½ cup chopped roasted salted almonds

1 tablespoon all-purpose flour

1 recipe Cocoa Streusel (see Chapter 6)

1. Preheat oven to 350°F and prepare 18 muffin cups with nonstick spray, or line with paper liners.
2. In a large bowl sift together the flour, cocoa powder, baking powder, baking soda, and salt. Once sifted, whisk in the brown sugar until evenly mixed.
3. In a separate bowl add the butter, vanilla, half-and-half, and eggs. Whisk until the mixture is well combined.
4. Make a well in the center of the dry ingredients and pour in the wet ingredients. With a wooden spoon or spatula, gently fold the mixture until just combined, about 10 strokes. Do not overmix. In a small bowl combine the chocolate chips, marshmallows, and almonds with the flour until the chips are coated. Pour the mixture into the batter and fold to evenly distribute, about 3 strokes.
5. Divide the batter evenly between the prepared muffin cups and top with the Cocoa Streusel. Bake for 18–20 minutes, or until the muffins spring back when gently pressed in the center and the tops are golden brown. Cool in the pan for 3 minutes, then remove the muffins from the pan to cool on a wire rack. Enjoy warm.

Gingerbread Crumble Muffins

Gingerbread cake is a staple during the winter and around the holidays. This year, make that gingerbread a little more exciting with this crispy, crumble-topped muffin version. This recipe has all the familiar flavors of gingerbread, the spices and rich treacle, but its easy-to-transport form is perfect for sharing! Whether you're running to a family gathering or work holiday party or just to a casual get-together with friends, this sophisticated muffin is sure to impress, especially when paired with some Cinnamon Walnut Cream Cheese Spread (see Chapter 5).

Yields 18 Muffins

2¾ cups all-purpose flour

2½ teaspoons baking soda

1 tablespoon ground ginger

1 teaspoon ground cinnamon

⅛ teaspoon ground cloves

½ teaspoon salt

¼ cup butter, melted and cooled

¼ cup vegetable or canola oil

⅔ cup packed dark brown sugar

2 large eggs

⅔ cup molasses

1⅓ cups buttermilk

1 recipe Streusel Crumble (see Chapter 6)

1. Preheat oven to 350°F and prepare 18 muffin cups with nonstick spray, or line with paper liners.
2. In a medium bowl sift together the flour, baking soda, ginger, cinnamon, cloves, and salt. Set aside.
3. In a large bowl combine the butter, oil, and brown sugar. Mix until smooth, then add the eggs one at a time, beating well after each addition. Whisk in the molasses until smooth.
4. Add the flour mixture alternately with the buttermilk to the molasses mixture, beginning and ending with the flour.
5. Divide the batter evenly between the prepared muffin cups and top with the Streusel Crumble. Bake for 15–20 minutes, or until the muffins spring back when gently pressed in the center and the tops are golden brown. Cool in the pan for 3 minutes, then remove the muffins from the pan to cool on a wire rack. Enjoy warm.

Orange Saffron Muffins

Saffron, the stigmas of saffron crocus flowers, has a clean, almost herbal flavor and a bold red color. Once steeped it imparts its perfume and color into whatever it is mixed with. Here the clean flavor of saffron is combined with fresh orange to create a muffin that is completely unexpected. While saffron is slightly grassy and herbal orange is fresh and sweet, the combination of the two is refreshing and delicious.

Yields 18 Muffins

¼ cup fresh orange juice

¼ teaspoon saffron threads

2 cups all-purpose flour

1 teaspoon baking powder

½ teaspoon baking soda

½ teaspoon salt

¼ teaspoon cinnamon

1 tablespoon orange zest

½ cup sugar

½ cup packed light brown sugar

⅓ cup butter, melted and cooled

1 teaspoon vanilla

½ cup buttermilk

2 eggs

1 recipe Orange Glaze (see Chapter 6)

1. Preheat oven to 350°F and prepare 18 muffin cups with nonstick spray, or line with paper liners.
2. In a small pot over medium heat add the orange juice until it just simmers. Remove from the heat and add the saffron threads. Steep until the liquid reaches room temperature.
3. In a large bowl sift together the flour, baking powder, baking soda, salt, and cinnamon. Once sifted, whisk in the orange zest and both sugars until evenly mixed.
4. In a separate bowl add the saffron-infused orange juice, melted butter, vanilla, buttermilk, and eggs. Whisk until the mixture is well combined.
5. Make a well in the center of the dry ingredients and pour in the wet ingredients. With a wooden spoon or spatula gently fold the mixture until just combined, about 10–12 strokes. Do not overmix.
6. Divide the batter evenly between the prepared muffin cups. Bake for 18–20 minutes, or until the muffins spring back when gently pressed in the center and the tops are golden brown. Cool in the pan for 3 minutes, then remove the muffins from the pan to a wire rack to cool to room temperature.
7. Dip the tops of the muffins into the warm Orange Glaze, allowing the excess to drip off. Place the muffins on a cooling rack and allow the glaze to set, about 1 hour, before serving.

Peanut Butter Cup Stuffed Muffins

This muffin is sure to bring out the kid in anyone! Inside this peanut butter–flavored muffin there is a delicious secret—a miniature peanut butter cup. To get the best possible peanut butter flavor, use high-quality, all-natural peanut butter and fresh peanut butter cups. If you want to make this decadent delight even more surprising, substitute chocolate kisses or even chocolate truffles for the peanut butter cups. It makes a tasty surprise even more special!

Yields 18 Muffins

2 cups all-purpose flour

1 teaspoon baking powder

½ teaspoon baking soda

½ teaspoon salt

¼ cup packed light brown sugar

½ cup sugar

¼ cup vegetable or canola oil

½ cup peanut butter, melted and cooled

1 teaspoon vanilla

¾ cup buttermilk

¼ cup sour cream

2 eggs

18 mini peanut butter cups

1 recipe Peanut Butter Drizzle (see Chapter 6)

1. Preheat oven to 350°F and prepare 18 muffin cups with nonstick spray, or line with paper liners.
2. In a large bowl sift together the flour, baking powder, baking soda, and salt. Once sifted, whisk in both the sugars until evenly mixed.
3. In a separate bowl add the oil, peanut butter, vanilla, buttermilk, sour cream, and eggs. Whisk until the mixture is well combined.
4. Make a well in the center of the dry ingredients and pour in the wet ingredients. With a wooden spoon or spatula, gently fold the mixture until just combined, about 10–12 strokes. Do not overmix.
5. Divide half the batter evenly between the prepared muffin cups. Place a peanut butter cup in the center of each muffin, then top with the remaining batter. Bake for 18–20 minutes, or until the muffins spring back when gently pressed in the center and the tops are golden brown. Cool in the pan for 3 minutes, then remove the muffins from the pan to a wire rack to cool to room temperature.
6. Once the muffins have cooled, prepare the Peanut Butter Drizzle and drizzle the glaze over the top. Allow the glaze to set, about 1 hour, before serving.

Chocolate Cornmeal Muffins

Texture is an important part of a good muffin, and the addition of cornmeal to this chocolate muffin recipe takes texture into unexpected, surprisingly delicious territory. There is just a little cornmeal here, which ensures that this muffin won't have a cornbread texture; instead the muffin has a unique chewy crumb that is flecked with little bits of crunchy cornmeal. Delicious!

Yields 18 Muffins

1½ cups all-purpose flour

¼ cup Dutch-processed cocoa

¼ cup cornmeal

1 cup sugar

1 teaspoon baking powder

½ teaspoon baking soda

½ teaspoon salt

½ cup vegetable or canola oil

1 teaspoon vanilla

1 cup buttermilk

2 eggs

2 ounces chocolate, melted

1. Preheat oven to 350°F and prepare 18 muffin cups with nonstick spray, or line with paper liners.
2. In a large bowl whisk together the flour, cocoa powder, cornmeal, sugar, baking powder, baking soda, and salt until evenly mixed.
3. In a separate bowl add the oil, vanilla, buttermilk, and eggs. Whisk until the mixture is well combined, then stir in the melted chocolate.
4. Make a well in the center of the dry ingredients and pour in the wet ingredients. With a wooden spoon or spatula, gently fold the mixture until just combined, about 10–12 strokes. Do not overmix.
5. Divide the batter evenly between the prepared muffin cups. Bake for 18–20 minutes, or until the muffins spring back when gently pressed and the tops of the muffin are dry. Cool in the pan for 3 minutes, then remove the muffins from the pan to a wire rack to cool to room temperature.

Chocolate Cornmeal Muffins

Vanilla Bean Apple Muffins

The surprising flavor combination of vanilla and apple is a wonderfully sweet and often overlooked taste. In this recipe, the sharp flavor of apples is tempered by the sweet vanilla, and the combination is just heavenly. Vanilla-bean paste can be found in most gourmet or high-end food stores and is sold in small jars. If you are not able to find vanilla-bean paste, just use the seeds of one vanilla bean instead.

Yields 18 Muffins

1½ cups all-purpose flour

½ cup whole-wheat flour

1¼ teaspoons baking powder

½ teaspoon baking soda

½ teaspoon salt

½ teaspoon cinnamon

¼ teaspoon cardamom

½ cup sugar

¼ cup packed light brown sugar

⅓ cup butter, melted and cooled

1 teaspoon vanilla-bean paste

¾ cup buttermilk

2 eggs

1 cup grated Granny Smith apple

1. Preheat oven to 350°F and prepare 18 muffin cups with nonstick spray, or line with paper liners.
2. In a large bowl sift together the all-purpose flour, whole-wheat flour, baking powder, baking soda, salt, cinnamon, and cardamom. Once sifted, whisk in both the sugars until evenly mixed.
3. In a separate bowl add the melted butter, vanilla-bean paste, buttermilk, and eggs. Whisk until the mixture is well combined.
4. Make a well in the center of the dry ingredients and pour in the wet ingredients. With a wooden spoon or spatula, gently fold the mixture until just combined, about 10 strokes. Do not overmix. Add the grated apple and fold to incorporate, about 3 strokes.
5. Divide the batter evenly between the prepared muffin cups. Bake for 18–20 minutes, or until the muffins spring back when gently pressed in the center and the tops are golden brown. Cool in the pan for 3 minutes, then remove the muffins from the pan to a wire rack to cool to room temperature.

Pomegranate Molasses Muffins

Pomegranate molasses is simply a reduction of pure pomegranate juice, which is readily available in most grocery stores. Once reduced, the flavor becomes concentrated and quite tangy, and it is perfect for swirling into pies, cakes, or, in this case, muffins! In this recipe a high-quality, moist dark brown sugar will enhance the pomegranate's naturally robust flavor and sweetness while adding a deeper layer of flavor.

Yields 18 Muffins

1 cup pomegranate juice

2 cups all-purpose flour

1 teaspoon baking powder

½ teaspoon baking soda

½ teaspoon salt

1 cup packed dark brown sugar

¼ cup butter, melted and cooled

1 teaspoon vanilla

1 cup milk

2 eggs

1. In a small saucepan over medium heat, add the pomegranate juice. Bring the juice to a boil, then reduce the heat to medium low and simmer until the juice is reduced to ¼ cup, about 15 minutes. Cool to room temperature.
2. Heat oven to 350°F and prepare 18 muffin cups with nonstick spray, or line with paper liners.
3. In a large bowl sift together the flour, baking powder, baking soda, and salt. Once sifted, whisk in the dark brown sugar until evenly mixed.
4. In a separate bowl add the reduced pomegranate juice, melted butter, vanilla, milk, and eggs. Whisk until the mixture is well combined.
5. Make a well in the center of the dry ingredients and pour in the wet ingredients. With a wooden spoon or spatula, gently fold the mixture until just combined, about 10–12 strokes. Do not overmix.
6. Divide the batter evenly between the prepared muffin cups. Bake for 18–20 minutes, or until the muffins spring back when gently pressed in the center and the tops are golden brown. Cool in the pan for 3 minutes, then remove the muffins from the pan to a wire rack to cool to room temperature.

CHAPTER 2

Hearty Fruits, Nuts, and Oats

Homemade muffins have a unique comforting quality, and ingredients like rolled oats, dried fruits, and toasted nuts have offered delicious flavors and genuine nutritious appeal for decades. Homemade, however, does not need to be ho-hum. You can dress up comforting, familiar flavors to make them more daring, exciting, and gourmet. Just using a variety of fruits, nuts, and grains in muffins flavored with exotic cheeses, citrus, and seeds can provide a wealth of familiar flavors with a cosmopolitan twist.

In this chapter, you'll find high-class flavor pairings like browned butter with toasty oats, sweet mission figs with walnuts, and sesame seeds with lime. Raisins are nice, but they have a lot more zing if they are soaked in spiced rum. Pecans are lovely, but if you douse them in a spiced candy coating they become practically irresistible. A little change can lead to a huge impact, and a muffin is a perfect showcase for these dramatic flavors.

So, if it's a sophisticated, satisfying muffin you crave then you're in the right place! Get ready to experiment with some hearty fruits, nuts, and oats.

Almond Coconut Muffins

Almond and coconut are a happy mix of tropical heaven. To really boost the overall coconut flavor of this muffin, and to showcase the nuttiness, this recipe calls for toasted coconut *and* coconut milk. Using both will really give you the full spectrum of the coconut's already delicious flavor. The almond taste in this recipe is slightly more subtle because it's added through the almond extract and almond flour, which adds a buttery texture to the muffin's crumb.

Yields 18 Muffins

1½ cups all-purpose flour

½ cup almond flour

1 teaspoon baking powder

½ teaspoon baking soda

½ teaspoon salt

1 cup sugar

1 teaspoon vanilla

¼ teaspoon almond extract

½ cup butter, melted and cooled

1 cup coconut milk

2 eggs

1 cup toasted coconut

1. Preheat oven to 350°F and prepare 18 muffin cups with nonstick spray, or line with paper liners.
2. In a large bowl whisk together the flour, almond flour, baking powder, baking soda, salt, and sugar until evenly mixed.
3. In a separate bowl add the vanilla, almond extract, butter, coconut milk, and eggs. Whisk until the mixture is well combined, then stir in the melted chocolate.
4. Make a well in the center of the dry ingredients and pour in the wet ingredients. With a wooden spoon or spatula, gently fold the mixture until just combined, about 10 strokes. Do not overmix. Add the toasted coconut and fold until just mixed, about 3–4 strokes.
5. Divide the batter evenly between the prepared muffin cups. Bake for 18–20 minutes, or until the muffins spring back when gently pressed and the tops of the muffin are dry. Cool in the pan for 3 minutes, then remove the muffins from the pan to a wire rack to cool to room temperature.

Apple and Date Muffins

Dried dates are sweet, sticky, and sophisticated when paired with other sharper-flavored fruits like apples. While these are good any time of day, the caramel flavor of dates makes them a wonderful addition to dessert where a robust flavor is wanted. Not only do they add plenty of flavor, but they give these muffins a beautiful chewy texture and help them stay moister longer. If you don't care for dates, feel free to substitute golden raisins here instead.

Yields 18 Muffins

1½ cups all-purpose flour

½ cup whole-wheat flour

¾ teaspoon baking powder

¾ teaspoon baking soda

½ teaspoon salt

½ teaspoon cinnamon

¼ teaspoon cardamom

1 cup packed light brown sugar

⅓ cup canola or vegetable oil

1 teaspoon vanilla

1 cup buttermilk

2 eggs

1 cup diced apple

½ cup finely chopped dates

1 recipe Oat and Pecan Crumble
(see Chapter 6)

1. Preheat oven to 350°F and prepare 18 muffin cups with nonstick spray, or line with paper liners.
2. In a large bowl sift together the flour, whole-wheat flour, baking powder, baking soda, salt, cinnamon, and cardamom. Once sifted, whisk in the brown sugar until evenly mixed.
3. In a separate bowl add the oil, vanilla, buttermilk, and eggs. Whisk until the mixture is well combined.
4. Make a well in the center of the dry ingredients and pour in the wet ingredients. With a wooden spoon or spatula, gently fold the mixture until just combined, about 10 strokes. Do not overmix. Add the apple and dates and fold to evenly distribute, about 3 strokes.
5. Divide the batter evenly between the prepared muffin cups and top with the Oat and Pecan Crumble. Bake for 18–20 minutes, or until the muffins spring back when gently pressed in the center and the tops are golden brown. Cool in the pan for 3 minutes, then remove the muffins from the pan to cool on a wire rack. Enjoy warm.

Banana Maple Granola Muffins

These muffins have a rustic look and a very hearty texture. Granola—a combination of oats, grains, sugar, and sometimes nuts—is usually eaten as a cereal or snack food but in this recipe that granola is used as a main ingredient. Be sure to use very ripe bananas to give your muffins the strongest and sweetest banana flavor possible.

Yields 18 Muffins

2 medium-sized ripe bananas, mashed (about 1 cup)

¼ cup buttermilk

¼ cup dark maple syrup

¼ cup butter, melted and cooled

1 egg

1 teaspoon vanilla

1 cup all-purpose flour

⅔ cup packed light brown sugar

¼ teaspoon cinnamon

½ teaspoon baking soda

¼ teaspoon baking powder

½ teaspoon salt

1½ cups granola

1. Preheat oven to 350°F and either spray a 12-cup muffin pan with nonstick spray, or line with paper liners.
2. In a medium bowl whisk together the banana, buttermilk, maple syrup, butter, egg, and vanilla. Set aside.
3. In a large bowl add the flour, brown sugar, cinnamon, baking soda, baking powder, and salt. Whisk until well combined.
4. Make a well in the center of the dry ingredients and pour in the wet ingredients. With a wooden spoon or spatula, gently fold the mixture until just combined, about 10 strokes. Do not overmix. Add 1 cup of the granola and fold to mix, about 2–3 strokes.
5. Divide the batter evenly between the prepared muffin cups. Top each muffin with the remaining granola and bake for 18–20 minutes, or until the muffins spring back when gently pressed in the center and the tops are golden brown. Cool in the pan for 3 minutes, then remove the muffins from the pan to a wire rack to cool to room temperature.

Banana Walnut Chocolate Chip Muffins

The only thing finer than a slice of banana walnut bread is a banana walnut muffin studded with little bits of chocolate! Here the humble banana bread is made over into a muffin that has all the spicy kick of the original, but comes in an individual serving. Be sure to use very ripe bananas and very fresh walnuts here for the best flavor. If you want to make this muffin even more amazing, feel free to add a half cup of dried cherries, cranberries, or even raisins.

Yields 18 Muffins

1½ cups sugar

½ cup vegetable oil

2 eggs, lightly beaten

2 medium-sized ripe bananas, mashed (about 1 cup)

1¾ cups all-purpose flour

1 teaspoon salt

1 teaspoon baking soda

½ teaspoon baking powder

¼ teaspoon nutmeg

¼ teaspoon allspice

¼ teaspoon cinnamon

⅛ teaspoon cloves

⅛ teaspoon cardamom

⅔ cup whole milk

½ cup mini chocolate chips

½ cup chopped walnuts

1. Preheat oven to 350°F and prepare 18 muffin cups with nonstick spray, or line with paper liners.
2. In a large bowl combine the sugar and oil. Add the eggs one at a time until they are completely mixed, then stir in the banana. Set aside.
3. In a separate bowl sift together the flour, salt, baking soda, baking powder, nutmeg, allspice, cinnamon, cloves, and cardamom.
4. Add the flour mixture alternately with the milk to the banana mixture, beginning and ending with the flour mixture. Fold in the chocolate chips and walnuts.
5. Divide the batter evenly between the prepared muffin cups. Bake for 18–20 minutes, or until the muffins spring back when gently pressed in the center and the tops are golden brown. Cool in the pan for 3 minutes, then remove the muffins from the pan to a wire rack to cool to room temperature.

Black Walnut and Fig Muffins

Dried figs have a sweet, honeyed flavor and a voluptuous texture. And, while they are delicious when eaten on their own, here they are paired with the distinct smoky, nutty flavor of black walnuts. The resulting muffin is packed with deep flavors and many delightful textures. If you are unable to find black walnuts, use regular walnuts that have been toasted in a 350°F oven for about 8–10 minutes.

Yields 18 Muffins

2 cups all-purpose flour

1 teaspoon baking powder

½ teaspoon baking soda

½ teaspoon salt

¼ teaspoon cinnamon

1 cup packed dark brown sugar

⅓ cup butter, melted and cooled

1 teaspoon vanilla

1 cup whole milk

2 eggs

½ cup chopped black walnuts

½ cup finely chopped dried figs

Fig Ricotta Spread, optional (see Chapter 5)

1. Preheat oven to 350°F and prepare 18 muffin cups with nonstick spray, or line with paper liners.
2. In a large bowl sift together the flour, baking powder, baking soda, salt, and cinnamon. Once sifted, whisk in the dark brown sugar until evenly mixed.
3. In a separate bowl add the melted butter, vanilla, milk, and eggs. Whisk until the mixture is well combined.
4. Make a well in the center of the dry ingredients and pour in the wet ingredients. With a wooden spoon or spatula, gently fold the mixture until just combined, about 10 strokes. Do not overmix. Add the walnuts and figs and fold to mix, about 3 strokes.
5. Divide the batter evenly between the prepared muffin cups. Bake for 18–20 minutes, or until the muffins spring back when gently pressed in the center and the tops are golden brown. Cool in the pan for 3 minutes, then remove the muffins from the pan to a wire rack to cool to room temperature. Top with Fig Ricotta Spread, if desired.

Brown Butter and Oat Muffins with Oat Streusel (see Chapter 6)

Brown Butter and Oat Muffins

Browned butter, with its wonderful nutty flavor and rich, inviting aroma, is a fantastic way to add an extra layer of flavor to most baked goods—especially to muffins! The brown sugar in this recipe works to enhance the brown butter, and the Oat Streusel on top gives the finished package a lovely rustic appearance, which is sure to strike a note with any gourmand.

Yields 18 Muffins

½ cup butter

1 cup rolled oats

1½ cups all-purpose flour

1 teaspoon baking powder

½ teaspoon baking soda

½ teaspoon salt

1 cup packed light brown sugar

1 teaspoon vanilla

¾ cup whole milk

2 eggs

1 recipe Oat Streusel (see Chapter 6)

1 recipe Brown Butter Spread, optional (see Chapter 5)

1. In a small saucepan over medium heat add the butter. Cook, stirring constantly, until the butter foams and turns a deep nut brown color, about 12 minutes. Remove from the heat and cool to room temperature.
2. Heat oven to 350°F and prepare 18 muffin cups with nonstick spray, or line with paper liners.
3. In a blender or food processor add ½ cup of the oats. Process until the oats are a fine powder.
4. In a large bowl sift together the ½ cup ground oats, flour, baking powder, baking soda, and salt. Once sifted, whisk in the brown sugar and remaining rolled oats until evenly mixed.
5. In a separate bowl add the browned butter, vanilla, milk, and eggs. Whisk until the mixture is well combined.
6. Make a well in the center of the dry ingredients and pour in the wet ingredients. With a wooden spoon or spatula, gently fold the mixture until just combined, about 10–12 strokes. Do not overmix.
7. Divide the batter evenly between the prepared muffin cups and top with the Oat Streusel. Bake for 18–20 minutes, or until the muffins spring back when gently pressed in the center and the tops are golden brown. Cool in the pan for 3 minutes, then remove the muffins from the pan to a wire rack to cool to room temperature. Serve with the Brown Butter Spread if desired.

Blueberry Crumb Muffins

Fresh, in-season blueberries are the secret to a delicious blueberry muffin. While some recipes may call for blueberries that have been frozen, if you want your muffins to really impress, fresh berries are a necessity. This luxurious blueberry muffin is taken over the top with a crisp streusel, which both adds additional texture and gives the finished muffins a rustic, homemade look. These savory treats are wonderful warm and also freeze beautifully.

Yields 18 Muffins

2 cups all-purpose flour

1 teaspoon baking powder

½ teaspoon baking soda

½ teaspoon salt

¼ teaspoon cinnamon

¼ teaspoon cardamom

¾ cup packed light brown sugar

¼ cup canola oil

1 cup buttermilk

1 egg

1 teaspoon vanilla

1 cup fresh, ripe blueberries

2 tablespoons all-purpose flour

1 recipe Brown Sugar Streusel (see Chapter 6)

1. Preheat oven to 350°F and prepare 18 muffin cups with nonstick spray, or line with paper liners.
2. In a large bowl sift together the flour, baking powder, baking soda, salt, cinnamon, and cardamom. Once sifted, whisk in the brown sugar until evenly mixed.
3. In a separate bowl add the oil, buttermilk, egg, and vanilla. Whisk until the mixture is well combined.
4. Make a well in the center of the dry ingredients and pour in the wet ingredients. With a wooden spoon or spatula, gently fold the mixture until just combined, about 10 strokes. Do not overmix. In a small bowl toss the blueberries with the flour, then add this mixture to the batter and fold to evenly distribute, about 3 strokes.
5. Divide the batter evenly between the prepared muffin cups and top with the Brown Sugar Streusel. Bake for 18–20 minutes, or until the muffins spring back when gently pressed in the center and the tops are golden brown. Cool in the pan for 3 minutes, then remove the muffins from the pan to cool on a wire rack. Enjoy warm.

Blueberry Ricotta Streusel Muffins

A bowl of fresh ricotta cheese topped with fresh berries and honey is the delicious treat that inspired this muffin. In this recipe the ricotta cheese is mixed into the batter, which guarantees a tender, moist muffin that has the delicate, milky flavor of ricotta. Topping this refined food is a refreshing lemon-flavored streusel that keeps these muffins from being too rich and adds a lovely aromatic touch.

Yields 18 Muffins

2 cups all-purpose flour

½ cup sugar

¼ cup packed light brown sugar

1 teaspoon baking powder

½ teaspoon baking soda

½ teaspoon salt

¼ cup butter, melted and cooled

1 teaspoon vanilla

½ cup buttermilk

½ cup ricotta cheese

1 tablespoon freshly grated lemon zest

2 eggs

1 cup fresh blueberries

1 tablespoon all-purpose flour

1 recipe Lemon Zest Streusel (see Chapter 6)

1. Preheat oven to 350°F and prepare 18 muffin cups with nonstick spray, or line with paper liners.
2. In a large bowl sift together the flour, sugar, brown sugar, baking powder, baking soda, and salt.
3. In a separate bowl add the butter, vanilla, buttermilk, ricotta cheese, lemon zest, and eggs. Whisk until the mixture is well combined.
4. Make a well in the center of the dry ingredients and pour in the wet ingredients. With a wooden spoon or spatula, gently fold the mixture until just combined, about 10 strokes. Do not overmix. In a small bowl toss the blueberries with the flour, then add this mixture to the batter and fold to evenly distribute, about 3 strokes.
5. Divide the batter evenly between the prepared muffin cups and top with the Lemon Zest Streusel. Bake for 18–20 minutes, or until the muffins spring back when gently pressed in the center and the tops are golden brown. Cool in the pan for 3 minutes, then remove the muffins from the pan to a wire rack to cool to room temperature.

Brandied Apple Muffins

Cooking apples before adding them to baked goods ensures that they are tender and fully cooked. Here the apples are cooked in a mixture of sugar and brandy that lends a level of richness to these muffins. The apples absorb the rich flavor of the brandy as they cook. And, rather than waste all that goodness, once the apples are cooked, some of the brandy is reserved for the muffins, too. If you are not a fan of brandy, feel free to substitute rum, bourbon, or even apple cider if you want to avoid alcohol.

Yields 18 Muffins

½ cup brandy

¼ cup sugar

1 Granny Smith apple, peeled, cored, and diced

2 cups all-purpose flour

1¼ teaspoons baking powder

½ teaspoon baking soda

½ teaspoon salt

½ teaspoon cinnamon

¼ teaspoon allspice

½ cup sugar

¼ cup packed light brown sugar

⅓ cup butter, melted and cooled

1 teaspoon vanilla

½ cup buttermilk

2 eggs

1. In a medium saucepan over medium heat, add the brandy, sugar, and apple. Bring the mixture to a boil, then reduce to a simmer and cook until the apples are tender, about 10 minutes. Strain the apples, reserving ¼ cup of the brandy, and cool to room temperature.
2. Preheat oven to 350°F and prepare 18 muffin cups with nonstick spray, or line with paper liners.
3. In a large bowl sift together the all-purpose flour, baking powder, baking soda, salt, cinnamon, and allspice. Once sifted, whisk in both the sugars until evenly mixed.
4. In a separate bowl add the reserved brandy, melted butter, vanilla, buttermilk, and eggs. Whisk until the mixture is well combined.
5. Make a well in the center of the dry ingredients and pour in the wet ingredients. With a wooden spoon or spatula, gently fold the mixture until just combined, about 10 strokes. Do not overmix. Add the apple and fold to incorporate, about 3 strokes.
6. Divide the batter evenly between the prepared muffin cups. Bake for 18–20 minutes, or until the muffins spring back when gently pressed in the center and the tops are golden brown. Cool in the pan for 3 minutes, then remove the muffins from the pan to a wire rack to cool to room temperature.

Chocolate Hazelnut Muffins

Thanks to the pleasing chocolate hazelnut spreads available, the combination of chocolate and hazelnut has become very popular. For this recipe this blend of flavors is mixed into the batter along with cocoa powder to create a chocolaty muffin with a subtle hazelnut finish. If you want even more hazelnut flavor, consider adding ½ cup of chopped, toasted hazelnuts to the batter.

Yields 18 Muffins

2 cups all-purpose flour

¼ cup Dutch-processed cocoa powder

1 teaspoon baking powder

¾ teaspoon baking soda

½ teaspoon salt

1 cup packed light brown sugar

⅓ cup canola or vegetable oil

½ cup chocolate hazelnut spread

1 teaspoon vanilla

¾ cup milk

2 eggs

1. Preheat oven to 350°F and prepare 18 muffin cups with nonstick spray, or line with paper liners.
2. In a large bowl sift together the flour, cocoa powder, baking powder, baking soda, and salt. Once sifted, whisk in the brown sugar until evenly mixed.
3. In a separate bowl add the oil, chocolate hazelnut spread, vanilla, milk, and eggs. Whisk until the mixture is well combined.
4. Make a well in the center of the dry ingredients and pour in the wet ingredients. With a wooden spoon or spatula, gently fold the mixture until just combined, about 10–12 strokes. Do not overmix.
5. Divide the batter evenly between the prepared muffin cups. Bake for 18–20 minutes, or until the muffins spring back when gently pressed in the center and the tops are golden brown. Cool in the pan for 3 minutes, then remove the muffins from the pan to cool on a wire rack. Enjoy warm.

Candied Pecan Muffins

Candied pecans, or pecans that are coated in a spiced sugar glaze, make a delicious snack all on their own. But here these candy-coated pecans are folded into the muffin batter, and scattered over the tops of these tender, moist treats. If you prefer, you could use almonds, walnuts, or even peanuts in this recipe, and you can adjust the spices to suit your tastes.

Yields 18 Muffins

1 large egg white

1½ cups packed light brown sugar, divided use

1½ teaspoons cinnamon, divided use

½ teaspoon nutmeg, divided use

1 teaspoon salt, divided use

2 cups pecan halves

2 cups all-purpose flour

1 teaspoon baking powder

¾ teaspoon baking soda

⅓ cup canola or vegetable oil

1 teaspoon vanilla

¾ cup buttermilk

2 eggs

1. Preheat oven to 350°F. Spray a rimmed baking sheet with nonstick cooking spray, and prepare 18 muffin cups with nonstick spray, or line with paper liners.
2. In a large bowl beat the egg white with a hand mixer until very frothy, about 30 seconds. Add ½ cup of the brown sugar, 1 teaspoon of the cinnamon, ¼ teaspoon of the nutmeg, and ½ teaspoon of the salt, and whisk until mixture thickens, about 1 minute. Add pecans and stir until evenly coated.
3. With a slotted spoon or with forks, transfer the nuts to the prepared baking sheet, making sure the nuts are evenly spaced. Bake nuts until golden brown, about 10–12 minutes. Cool completely on the baking sheet, then roughly chop. Set aside.
4. In a large bowl sift together the flour, baking powder, baking soda, remaining ½ teaspoon of salt, remaining ½ teaspoon of cinnamon, and remaining ¼ teaspoon of nutmeg. Once sifted, whisk in the brown sugar until evenly mixed.
5. In a separate bowl add the oil, vanilla, buttermilk, and eggs. Whisk until the mixture is well combined.
6. Make a well in the center of the dry ingredients and pour in the wet ingredients. With a wooden spoon or spatula, gently fold the mixture until just combined, about 10 strokes. Do not overmix. Add two-thirds of the chopped pecans into the batter and fold to evenly distribute, about 3 strokes.
7. Divide the batter evenly between the prepared muffin cups and top with the remaining pecans. Bake for 18–20 minutes, or until the muffins spring back when gently pressed in the center and the tops are golden brown. Cool in the pan for 3 minutes, then remove the muffins from the pan to cool on a wire rack. Enjoy warm.

Candied Pecan Muffins

Peach Pecan Streusel Muffins

Peaches and pecans make for a perfect pairing. Whereas the peaches are sweet and tangy, the pecans are buttery and rich; their differences are what make them so good together. In this recipe the peach muffin is flecked with chopped pecans and topped with an irresistible Streusel Crumble. Here, peach nectar is used to pump up the peach flavor, but if you prefer you can also use fresh peach purée thinned down with a little water.

Yields 18 Muffins

2 cups all-purpose flour

1 teaspoon baking powder

¾ teaspoon baking soda

½ teaspoon salt

¼ teaspoon cinnamon

1 cup packed sugar

⅓ cup canola or vegetable oil

1 teaspoon vanilla

½ cup buttermilk

¼ cup peach nectar

2 eggs

2 peaches, peeled, pitted, and diced

½ cup chopped pecans

1 recipe Streusel Crumble (see Chapter 6)

1. Preheat oven to 350°F and prepare 18 muffin cups with nonstick spray, or line with paper liners.
2. In a large bowl sift together the flour, baking powder, baking soda, salt, and cinnamon. Once sifted, whisk in the sugar until evenly mixed.
3. In a separate bowl add the oil, vanilla, buttermilk, peach nectar, and eggs. Whisk until the mixture is well combined.
4. Make a well in the center of the dry ingredients and pour in the wet ingredients. With a wooden spoon or spatula, gently fold the mixture until just combined, about 10 strokes. Do not overmix. Add the diced peaches and pecans into the batter and fold to evenly distribute, about 3 strokes.
5. Divide the batter evenly between the prepared muffin cups and top with the Streusel Crumble. Bake for 18–20 minutes, or until the muffins spring back when gently pressed in the center and the tops are golden brown. Cool in the pan for 3 minutes, then remove the muffins from the pan to cool on a wire rack. Enjoy warm.

Fresh Blueberry Compote Sour Cream Muffins

Blueberry compote is a delicious combination of fresh blueberries, sugar, and citrus that is cooked down and thickened. It is similar to a fresh jam and adds lovely swirls of blue to this beautiful muffin. But as pretty as this muffin is to look at, it is even better to taste. The sour cream added to the batter gives this *moufflet* a rich, sharp flavor that pairs well with the sweet blueberries. You could also make this recipe with cherries if you like.

Yields 18 Muffins

1½ cups fresh blueberries

1 tablespoon cornstarch

2 tablespoons sugar

1 tablespoon water

1 tablespoon fresh lime juice

2 cups all-purpose flour

1 teaspoon baking powder

¾ teaspoon baking soda

½ teaspoon salt

1 cup sugar

⅓ cup butter, melted and cooled

1 teaspoon vanilla

½ cup sour cream

¼ cup half-and-half

2 eggs

1. In a medium saucepan mix 1 cup of the blueberries, the cornstarch, sugar, water, and lime juice. Cook over medium-low heat, stirring constantly, until thick and the berries have burst, about 10 minutes. Let the mixture cool to room temperature, then fold in the remaining blueberries.

2. Preheat oven to 350°F and prepare 18 muffin cups with nonstick spray, or line with paper liners.

3. In a large bowl sift together the flour, baking powder, baking soda, and salt. Once sifted, whisk in the sugar until evenly mixed.

4. In a separate bowl add the butter, vanilla, sour cream, half-and-half, and eggs. Whisk until the mixture is well combined.

5. Make a well in the center of the dry ingredients and pour in the wet ingredients. With a wooden spoon or spatula, gently fold the mixture until just combined, about 10 strokes. Do not overmix. Add half the blueberry mixture and just swirl it into the batter, leaving large streaks of blueberry.

6. Divide half the batter evenly between the prepared muffin cups, and top with the reserved blueberry compote. Then top with the remaining batter. Bake for 18–20 minutes, or until the muffins spring back when gently pressed in the center and the tops are golden brown. Cool in the pan for 3 minutes, then remove the muffins from the pan to cool on a wire rack. Enjoy warm.

Cranberry Orange Streusel Muffins

Freshly squeezed orange juice and tangy cranberries make this muffin an especially refined treat. The orange juice is used to plump up the dry cranberries so orange flavor is present in every part of this *moufflet*. The streusel topping gives these muffins a huge boost in flavor and takes this recipe from day-to-day to deliciously decadent!

Yields 18 Muffins

1 cup fresh orange juice

1 cup dried cranberries

2 cups all-purpose flour

1 teaspoon baking powder

¾ teaspoon baking soda

½ teaspoon salt

¼ teaspoon cinnamon

1 cup packed light brown sugar

⅓ cup canola or vegetable oil

1 teaspoon vanilla

1 tablespoon orange zest

¾ cup buttermilk

2 eggs

1 recipe Streusel Crumble (see Chapter 6)

1. In a small saucepan over medium heat, add the orange juice and cranberries. Bring to a boil, then remove from the heat and allow to cool to room temperature. Strain the cranberries.

2. Preheat oven to 350°F and prepare 18 muffin cups with nonstick spray, or line with paper liners.

3. In a large bowl sift together the flour, baking powder, baking soda, salt, and cinnamon. Once sifted, whisk in the brown sugar until evenly mixed.

4. In a separate bowl add the oil, vanilla, orange zest, buttermilk, and eggs. Whisk until the mixture is well combined.

5. Make a well in the center of the dry ingredients and pour in the wet ingredients. With a wooden spoon or spatula, gently fold the mixture until just combined, about 10 strokes. Do not overmix. Add the cranberries into the batter and fold to evenly distribute, about 3 strokes.

6. Divide the batter evenly between the prepared muffin cups and top with the Streusel Crumble. Bake for 18–20 minutes, or until the muffins spring back when gently pressed in the center and the tops are golden brown. Cool in the pan for 3 minutes, then remove the muffins from the pan to cool on a wire rack. Enjoy warm.

Orange Almond Muffins

Almond and orange are the primary ingredients in a popular Middle Eastern cake that inspired this amazing muffin. The sharp citrus and mild almond flavors complement each other without being too strong and, while the traditional cake is flourless, the flour in these muffins gives them a much lighter texture.

Yields 18 Muffins

1½ cups all-purpose flour

½ cup almond meal or almond flour

1 teaspoon baking powder

½ teaspoon baking soda

½ teaspoon salt

1 cup sugar

1 teaspoon vanilla

¼ teaspoon almond extract

1 tablespoon orange zest

½ cup butter, melted and cooled

1 cup buttermilk

2 eggs

1 recipe Almond Brown Sugar Topping (see Chapter 6)

1. Preheat oven to 350°F and prepare 18 muffin cups with nonstick spray, or line with paper liners.
2. In a large bowl whisk together the flour, almond flour, baking powder, baking soda, salt, and sugar until evenly mixed.
3. In a separate bowl add the vanilla, almond extract, orange zest, melted butter, buttermilk, and eggs. Whisk until the mixture is well combined.
4. Make a well in the center of the dry ingredients and pour in the wet ingredients. With a wooden spoon or spatula, gently fold the mixture until just combined, about 10 strokes. Do not overmix.
5. Divide the batter evenly between the prepared muffin cups and top with the Almond Brown Sugar Topping. Bake for 18–20 minutes, or until the muffins spring back when gently pressed and the tops of the muffin are dry. Cool in the pan for 3 minutes, then remove the muffins from the pan to a wire rack to cool to room temperature.

Chocolate Cherry Swirl Muffins

Chocolate-covered cherries are often thought of as a guilty pleasure and this muffin borrows those flavors for these tasty chocolate muffins swirled with sweet cherry. To ensure that you get the best flavor, look for a cherry preserve that has whole fruit in it; the little bits of cherry will give your muffins more texture and more flavor.

Yields 18 Muffins

2 cups all-purpose flour

1 teaspoon baking powder

½ teaspoon baking soda

½ teaspoon salt

1 cup sugar

½ cup butter, melted and cooled

1 teaspoon vanilla

¾ cup buttermilk

2 eggs

2 tablespoons Dutch-processed cocoa

¼ cup cherry preserves

1. Preheat oven to 350°F and prepare 18 muffin cups with nonstick spray, or line with paper liners.
2. In a large bowl sift together the flour, baking powder, baking soda, and salt. Once sifted, whisk in the sugar until evenly mixed.
3. In a separate bowl add the melted butter, vanilla, buttermilk, and eggs. Whisk until the mixture is well combined.
4. Make a well in the center of the dry ingredients and pour in the wet ingredients. With a wooden spoon or spatula, gently fold the mixture until just combined, about 10 strokes. Do not overmix.
5. Divide the batter into two bowls. Into one add the cocoa powder, into the other add the cherry preserves. Mix both until they are evenly mixed, about 5–8 strokes.
6. Spoon half the chocolate batter into the prepared muffin cups. Next add the cherry batter, then top with the remaining chocolate batter. With a butter knife, make a figure–eight pattern in each muffin one time. Bake for 18–20 minutes, or until the muffins spring back when gently pressed in the center and the tops are golden brown. Cool in the pan for 3 minutes, then remove the muffins from the pan to a wire rack to cool to room temperature.

Chocolate Cherry Swirl Muffins

Pumpkin and Toasted Oat Muffins

Typical oat muffins are pretty tasty, but usually a little bit boring. Here the humble oat gets a boost of flavor from a simple technique—toasting! Toasting the oats before adding them to the batter gives them a richer, earthier flavor and enhances their texture. When combined with the pumpkin purée, these ingredients create a hearty, yet pleasantly different muffin that will impress your guests and keep people coming back for more!

Yields 18 Muffins

⅔ cup rolled oats

1½ cups all-purpose flour

1 teaspoon baking powder

½ teaspoon baking soda

1 teaspoon cinnamon

⅛ teaspoon cloves

⅛ teaspoon fresh ground nutmeg

¼ teaspoon allspice

½ teaspoon salt

¾ cup packed light brown sugar

1 egg

1 teaspoon vanilla

1 cup pumpkin purée

⅓ cup unsalted butter, melted and cooled

⅓ cup buttermilk

1. Preheat oven to 350°F and prepare 18 muffin cups with nonstick spray, or line with paper liners.
2. On a baking sheet spread the oats into an even layer. Bake, stirring often, until the oats are golden brown, about 10 minutes. Allow to cool completely.
3. In a large bowl sift together the flour, baking powder, baking soda, cinnamon, cloves, nutmeg, allspice, and salt. Once sifted, whisk in the toasted oats and brown sugar until evenly mixed.
4. In a separate bowl add the egg, vanilla, pumpkin purée, butter, and buttermilk. Whisk until the mixture is well combined.
5. Make a well in the center of the dry ingredients and pour in the wet ingredients. With a wooden spoon or spatula, gently fold the mixture until just combined, about 10–12 strokes. Do not overmix.
6. Divide the batter evenly between the prepared muffin cups. Bake for 18–20 minutes, or until the muffins spring back when gently pressed in the center and the tops are golden brown. Cool in the pan for 3 minutes, then remove the muffins from the pan to cool on a wire rack. Enjoy warm.

Raspberry Lemon Muffins

Fresh raspberries are a delicious, tempting, springtime treat—whether you're eating them fresh off the bush or incorporating them into this fresh muffin recipe! Here, raspberry is paired with the bright citrus flavor of lemon, which adds a little edge to the natural flavors of the sweet raspberry. To gild the lily just a little bit more, the muffins are covered in a sophisticated Limoncello Glaze.

Yields 18 Muffins

2 cups all-purpose flour

1 teaspoon baking powder

½ teaspoon baking soda

½ teaspoon salt

¾ cup sugar

¼ cup butter, melted and cooled

2 tablespoons vegetable or canola oil

1 teaspoon vanilla

1 tablespoon freshly grated lemon zest

1 cup buttermilk

2 eggs

1 cup fresh raspberries

1 recipe Limoncello Glaze (see Chapter 6)

1. Preheat oven to 350°F and prepare 18 muffin cups with nonstick spray, or line with paper liners.
2. In a large bowl sift together the flour, baking powder, baking soda, and salt. Once sifted, whisk in the sugar until evenly mixed.
3. In a separate bowl add the melted butter, oil, vanilla, lemon zest, buttermilk, and eggs. Whisk until the mixture is well combined.
4. Make a well in the center of the dry ingredients and pour in the wet ingredients. With a wooden spoon or spatula, gently fold the mixture until just combined, about 10 strokes. Do not overmix. Gently fold in the raspberries, about 3 strokes.
5. Divide the batter evenly between the prepared muffin cups. Bake for 18–20 minutes, or until the muffins spring back when gently pressed in the center and the tops are golden brown. Cool in the pan for 3 minutes, then remove the muffins from the pan to a wire rack to cool to room temperature.
6. Once the muffins have cooled, prepare the Limoncello Glaze. Dip the tops of the muffins into the warm glaze, allowing the excess to drip off. Place the muffins on a cooling rack and allow the glaze to set, about 1 hour, before serving.

Strawberries and Cream Muffins

If you find strawberry shortcake hard to resist, then these sophisticated strawberry muffins are perfect for you! The muffin itself is moist, rich, and loaded with bits of fresh strawberry. The richness comes from heavy cream and half-and-half, both of which are used in this recipe. These muffins are a welcome addition to any breakfast table, but are also good as a dessert topped with a little fresh whipped cream.

Yields 18 Muffins

2 cups all-purpose flour

1 teaspoon baking powder

½ teaspoon baking soda

½ teaspoon salt

½ cup sugar

¼ cup packed light brown sugar

⅓ cup vegetable or canola oil

1 teaspoon vanilla

½ cup half-and-half

½ cup heavy cream

2 eggs

1 cup diced fresh strawberries

1. Preheat oven to 350°F and prepare 18 muffin cups with nonstick spray, or line with paper liners.
2. In a large bowl sift together the flour, baking powder, baking soda, and salt. Once sifted, whisk in both the sugars until evenly mixed.
3. In a separate bowl add the oil, vanilla, half-and-half, heavy cream, and eggs. Whisk until the mixture is well combined.
4. Make a well in the center of the dry ingredients and pour in the wet ingredients. With a wooden spoon or spatula, gently fold the mixture until just combined, about 10 strokes. Do not overmix. Gently fold in the strawberries, about 3 strokes.
5. Divide the batter evenly between the prepared muffin cups. Bake for 18–20 minutes, or until the muffins spring back when gently pressed in the center and the tops are golden brown. Cool in the pan for 3 minutes, then remove the muffins from the pan to a wire rack to cool to room temperature.

Strawberry Champagne Muffins

Champagne may seem like an extravagant ingredient, but the flavor and lightness it lends to these muffins make it worth it! With its effervescent bubbles and its sharply sweet flavor, champagne adds a real kick to these strawberry delicacies. If you prefer to avoid alcohol you can substitute sparkling apple cider, ginger ale, or even club soda for the champagne.

Yields 18 Muffins

2 cups all-purpose flour

1 teaspoon baking powder

½ teaspoon baking soda

½ teaspoon salt

¾ cup sugar

⅓ cup vegetable or canola oil

¼ cup strawberry preserves, melted and cooled

1 teaspoon vanilla

¼ cup whole milk

½ cup champagne or sparkling wine

2 eggs

2–3 drops red food coloring, optional

1 cup diced fresh strawberries

1. Preheat oven to 350°F and prepare 18 muffin cups with nonstick spray, or line with paper liners.
2. In a large bowl sift together the flour, baking powder, baking soda, and salt. Once sifted, whisk in the sugar until evenly mixed.
3. In a separate bowl add the oil, strawberry preserves, vanilla, milk, champagne, eggs, and red food coloring. Whisk until the mixture is well combined.
4. Make a well in the center of the dry ingredients and pour in the wet ingredients. With a wooden spoon or spatula, gently fold the mixture until just combined, about 10 strokes. Do not overmix. Gently fold in the strawberries, about 3 strokes.
5. Divide the batter evenly between the prepared muffin cups. Bake for 18–20 minutes, or until the muffins spring back when gently pressed in the center and the tops are golden brown. Cool in the pan for 3 minutes, then remove the muffins from the pan to a wire rack to cool to room temperature.

Coconut Glazed Pineapple Muffins

Coconut Glazed Pineapple Muffins

A tropical escape is just moments away with this sweet, yet refreshing muffin. Crushed pineapple and shredded coconut are folded into the batter, and then the finished muffins are glazed with an aromatic coconut glaze. To make these muffins even more attractive, consider adding a sprinkle of toasted coconut over the tops when the glaze is still wet.

Yields 18 Muffins

2 cups all-purpose flour

¾ teaspoon baking powder

¾ teaspoon baking soda

½ teaspoon salt

1 cup packed light brown sugar

⅓ cup canola or vegetable oil

1 teaspoon vanilla

¼ teaspoon coconut extract

¾ cup buttermilk

2 eggs

1 cup drained crushed pineapple

½ cup shredded coconut

1 recipe Coconut Glaze (see Chapter 6)

1. Preheat oven to 350°F and prepare 18 muffin cups with nonstick spray, or line with paper liners.
2. In a large bowl sift together the flour, baking powder, baking soda, and salt. Once sifted, whisk in the brown sugar until evenly mixed.
3. In a separate bowl add the oil, vanilla, coconut extract, buttermilk, and eggs. Whisk until the mixture is well combined.
4. Make a well in the center of the dry ingredients and pour in the wet ingredients. With a wooden spoon or spatula, gently fold the mixture until just combined, about 10 strokes. Do not overmix. Add the pineapple and coconut into the batter, and fold to evenly distribute, about 3–4 strokes.
5. Divide the batter evenly between the prepared muffin cups. Bake for 18–20 minutes, or until the muffins spring back when gently pressed in the center and the tops are golden brown. Cool in the pan for 3 minutes, then remove the muffins from the pan to cool on a wire rack.
6. Once the muffins have cooled, prepare the Coconut Glaze. Dip the tops of the muffins into the warm glaze, allowing the excess to drip off. Place the muffins on a cooling rack and allow the glaze to set, about 1 hour, before serving.

Whole-Wheat Banana Pecan Muffins

The ripe banana, cinnamon, pecans, and the Oat and Pecan Crumble that tops off this recipe really make this *moufflet* more than amazing. But this muffin doesn't just taste good, it's good for you! The whole-wheat flour in this recipe is full of fiber and nutrients and its nuttiness cannot be rivaled. Looks like you really can have your *moufflet*—and eat it too!

Yields 18 Muffins

2 medium-sized ripe bananas, mashed (about 1 cup)

¾ cup buttermilk

½ cup butter, melted and cooled

1 egg

1 egg white

1 teaspoon vanilla

1 cup all-purpose flour

1 cup whole-wheat flour

2 tablespoons wheat germ

¾ cup packed dark brown sugar

½ teaspoon cinnamon

1 teaspoon baking soda

½ teaspoon baking powder

¼ teaspoon salt

1 cup chopped pecans

1 recipe Oat and Pecan Crumble (see Chapter 6)

1. Preheat oven to 350°F and either spray a 12-cup muffin pan with nonstick spray or line with paper liners.
2. In a medium bowl whisk together the bananas, buttermilk, butter, egg, egg white, and vanilla. Set aside.
3. In a large bowl add the flour, whole-wheat flour, wheat germ, brown sugar, cinnamon, baking soda, baking powder, and salt. Whisk until well combined.
4. Make a well in the center of the dry ingredients and pour in the wet ingredients. With a wooden spoon or spatula, gently fold the mixture until just combined, about 10 strokes. Do not overmix. Add the pecans and fold to mix, about 2–3 strokes.
5. Divide the batter evenly between the prepared muffin cups. Top each muffin with the Oat and Pecan Crumble and bake for 18–20 minutes, or until the muffins spring back when gently pressed in the center and the tops are golden brown. Cool in the pan for 3 minutes, then remove the muffins from the pan to a wire rack to cool. Serve warm.

Cinnamon Buttermilk Muffins

Warm cinnamon is a very comforting, familiar flavor that deserves to be the star of a dish. Here, in these decadent muffins, the much-loved flavor of cinnamon gets a chance to shine. These streusel-topped muffins make a great snack, breakfast, or even dessert. Make them even more dazzling by dressing them up with a little ice cream or even a drizzle of caramel sauce.

Yields 18 Muffins

2 cups all-purpose flour

1 teaspoon baking powder

½ teaspoon baking soda

½ teaspoon cinnamon

¼ teaspoon allspice

½ teaspoon salt

1 cup packed light brown sugar

⅓ cup butter, melted and cooled

1 teaspoon vanilla

1 cup buttermilk

2 eggs

1 recipe Brown Sugar Streusel (see Chapter 6)

1. Preheat oven to 350°F and prepare 18 muffin cups with nonstick spray, or line with paper liners.
2. In a large bowl sift together the flour, baking powder, baking soda, cinnamon, allspice, and salt. Once sifted, whisk in the brown sugar until evenly mixed.
3. In a separate bowl add the melted butter, vanilla, buttermilk, and eggs. Whisk until the mixture is well combined.
4. Make a well in the center of the dry ingredients and pour in the wet ingredients. With a wooden spoon or spatula, gently fold the mixture until just combined, about 10–12 strokes. Do not overmix.
5. Divide the batter evenly between the prepared muffin cups and top with the Brown Sugar Streusel. Bake for 18–20 minutes, or until the muffins spring back when gently pressed in the center and the tops are golden brown. Cool in the pan for 3 minutes, then remove the muffins from the pan to a wire rack to cool to room temperature.

Rum-Soaked Raisin Muffins

Dark rum has a caramel flavor that pairs amazingly well with dried fruit like the golden raisins found in this recipe. If you don't care for rum, feel free to substitute bourbon or even apple cider without sacrificing any of the delicious flavor.

Yields 18 Muffins

1 cup dark rum

1 cup golden raisins

2 cups all-purpose flour

1 teaspoon baking powder

¾ teaspoon baking soda

½ teaspoon salt

¼ teaspoon cinnamon

1 cup packed light brown sugar

⅓ cup canola or vegetable oil

1 teaspoon vanilla

¾ cup buttermilk

2 eggs

1. In a small saucepan over medium heat add the rum and raisins. Bring to a boil, then remove from the heat and allow to cool to room temperature. Strain the raisins and reserve ¼ cup of the rum.
2. Preheat oven to 350°F and prepare 18 muffin cups with nonstick spray, or line with paper liners.
3. In a large bowl sift together the flour, baking powder, baking soda, salt, and cinnamon. Once sifted, whisk in the brown sugar until evenly mixed.
4. In a separate bowl add the reserved rum, the oil, vanilla, buttermilk, and eggs. Whisk until the mixture is well combined.
5. Make a well in the center of the dry ingredients and pour in the wet ingredients. With a wooden spoon or spatula, gently fold the mixture until just combined, about 10 strokes. Do not overmix. Add the raisins and fold to evenly distribute, about 2–3 strokes.
6. Divide the batter evenly between the prepared muffin cups and bake for 18–20 minutes, or until the muffins spring back when gently pressed in the center and the tops are golden brown. Cool in the pan for 3 minutes, then remove the muffins from the pan to cool on a wire rack. Enjoy warm.

Rum-Soaked Raisin Muffins

Ginger Pear Muffins

The spicy flavor of ginger adds tremendous flavor to sweets. While powdered ginger is a fine choice, freshly grated ginger adds even more flavorful dimensions. Here the heat of the freshly grated ginger is juxtaposed with the mild, sweet flavor of bits of fresh pear. How can you say no?

Yields 18 Muffins

2 cups all-purpose flour

1¼ teaspoons baking powder

½ teaspoon baking soda

½ teaspoon salt

¼ teaspoon cardamom

¾ cup sugar

⅓ cup butter, melted and cooled

1 teaspoon vanilla

¼ cup freshly grated ginger

1 tablespoon freshly grated lemon zest

½ cup buttermilk

¼ cup pear nectar

2 eggs

1 Bosc pear, peeled, cored, and diced

1. Preheat oven to 350°F and prepare 18 muffin cups with nonstick spray, or line with paper liners.
2. In a large bowl sift together the flour, baking powder, baking soda, salt, and cardamom. Once sifted, whisk in the sugar until evenly mixed.
3. In a separate bowl add the melted butter, vanilla, ginger, lemon zest, buttermilk, pear nectar, and eggs. Whisk until the mixture is well combined.
4. Make a well in the center of the dry ingredients and pour in the wet ingredients. With a wooden spoon or spatula, gently fold the mixture until just combined, about 10 strokes. Do not overmix. Add the diced pear and fold to incorporate, about 3 strokes.
5. Divide the batter evenly between the prepared muffin cups. Bake for 18–20 minutes, or until the muffins spring back when gently pressed in the center and the tops are golden brown. Cool in the pan for 3 minutes, then remove the muffins from the pan to a wire rack to cool to room temperature.

Orange Pistachio Muffins

Finely grinding pistachios is a way to add moisture, flavor, and a unique texture to these irresistible muffins. Because the pistachios are ground, their flavor is evenly distributed throughout the muffin so each bite has the right balance of buttery nuts and crisp orange. These are lovely served with tea and some freshly whipped honey butter.

Yields 18 Muffins

1½ cups chopped pistachios

2 cups all-purpose flour

1¼ teaspoons baking powder

½ teaspoon baking soda

½ teaspoon salt

¾ cup sugar

⅓ cup butter, melted and cooled

1 teaspoon vanilla

1 tablespoon freshly grated orange zest

¾ cup buttermilk

2 eggs

1. Preheat oven to 350°F and prepare 18 muffin cups with nonstick spray, or line with paper liners.
2. In a food processor grind ½ cup of the pistachios until they are the texture of sand.
3. In a large bowl sift together the flour, baking powder, baking soda, and salt. Once sifted, whisk in the ground pistachios and sugar until evenly mixed.
4. In a separate bowl add the melted butter, vanilla, orange zest, buttermilk, and eggs. Whisk until the mixture is well combined.
5. Make a well in the center of the dry ingredients and pour in the wet ingredients. With a wooden spoon or spatula, gently fold the mixture until just combined, about 10 strokes. Do not overmix. Add the remaining pistachios and fold to incorporate, about 3 strokes.
6. Divide the batter evenly between the prepared muffin cups. Bake for 18–20 minutes, or until the muffins spring back when gently pressed in the center and the tops are golden brown. Cool in the pan for 3 minutes, then remove the muffins from the pan to a wire rack to cool to room temperature.

Fruitcake Muffins

Although fruitcake catches a bad rap, these muffins take the flavors in this popular cake from ho-hum hostess gift to hot-from-the-oven holiday favorite! Rather than use the neon-colored candied fruits that are common to the cake, these muffins use dried fruits like tangy cherries, sweet dates, and rich golden raisins. So forget the hostess gift. These muffins are too delicious to share!

Yields 18 Muffins

½ cup dried cherries

½ cup chopped dried dates

¼ cup golden raisins

1 cup bourbon

½ cup water

¼ cup sugar

2 cups all-purpose flour

1¼ teaspoons baking powder

½ teaspoon baking soda

½ teaspoon salt

½ teaspoon cinnamon

¼ teaspoon cloves

½ cup packed dark brown sugar

⅓ cup butter, melted and cooled

1 teaspoon vanilla

¼ cup molasses

1 tablespoon freshly grated orange zest

½ cup milk

2 eggs

½ cup chopped walnuts

1. In a medium saucepan over medium heat add the dried cherries and dates, the raisins, bourbon, water, and sugar. Bring to a boil, then turn off the heat and allow the mixture to cool to room temperature. Strain the fruit and reserve ¼ cup of the liquid.
2. Preheat oven to 350°F and prepare 18 muffin cups with nonstick spray, or line with paper liners.
3. In a large bowl sift together the flour, baking powder, baking soda, salt, cinnamon, and cloves. Once sifted, whisk in the dark brown sugar until evenly mixed.
4. In a separate bowl add the reserved bourbon, melted butter, vanilla, molasses, orange zest, milk, and eggs. Whisk until the mixture is well combined.
5. Make a well in the center of the dry ingredients and pour in the wet ingredients. With a wooden spoon or spatula, gently fold the mixture until just combined, about 10 strokes. Do not overmix. Add the fruit and walnuts and fold to incorporate, about 3 strokes.
6. Divide the batter evenly between the prepared muffin cups. Bake for 18–20 minutes, or until the muffins spring back when gently pressed in the center and the tops are golden brown. Cool in the pan for 3 minutes, then remove the muffins from the pan to a wire rack to cool to room temperature.

Peach Oat Flour Muffins

Peaches are velvety and sweet, and they pair very well with hearty grains and oats. This muffin uses home-milled oat flour to add an oat flavor without adding large pieces of oat to the muffin. Making oat flour is very easy, and the texture and flavor it adds are well worth the effort. For the best texture it is best to use peaches that are not quite ripe; they will retain their texture better after baking.

Yields 18 Muffins

⅔ cup rolled oats

1¼ cups all-purpose flour

1 teaspoon baking powder

½ teaspoon baking soda

¼ teaspoon cinnamon

½ teaspoon salt

¾ cup sugar

2 eggs

1 teaspoon vanilla

⅓ cup unsalted butter, melted and cooled

⅓ cup buttermilk

¼ cup whole milk yogurt

2 peaches, peeled, pitted, and diced

1. Preheat oven to 350°F and prepare 18 muffin cups with nonstick spray, or line with paper liners.
2. In a food processor or blender, add the oats and process until they form a fine powder.
3. In a large bowl sift together the ground oats, flour, baking powder, baking soda, cinnamon, and salt. Once sifted, whisk in the ground oats and sugar until evenly mixed.
4. In a separate bowl add the eggs, vanilla, butter, buttermilk, and yogurt. Whisk until the mixture is well combined.
5. Make a well in the center of the dry ingredients and pour in the wet ingredients. With a wooden spoon or spatula, gently fold the mixture until just combined, about 10 strokes. Do not overmix. Add the diced peaches and fold to combine, about 3 strokes.
6. Divide the batter evenly between the prepared muffin cups. Bake for 18–20 minutes, or until the muffins spring back when gently pressed in the center and the tops are golden brown. Cool in the pan for 3 minutes, then remove the muffins from the pan to cool on a wire rack. Enjoy warm.

White Chocolate Cranberry Banana Muffins

White Chocolate Cranberry Banana Muffins

These banana muffins are loaded with little bits of heaven in the form of dry cranberries and smooth white chocolate chips. While banana and cranberry are a common combination, adding just a little white chocolate makes these muffins unexpected, upscale, and oh so good! If you prefer you could substitute semisweet chips for the white chocolate, or use a combination of the two for an even more exotic treat!

Yields 18 Muffins

2 medium-sized ripe bananas, mashed (about 1 cup)

¾ cup buttermilk

½ cup butter, melted and cooled

1 egg

1 teaspoon vanilla

1½ cups all-purpose flour

¾ cup sugar

½ teaspoon cinnamon

1 teaspoon baking soda

½ teaspoon baking powder

¼ teaspoon salt

½ cup dry cranberries

½ cup white chocolate chips

1. Preheat oven to 350°F and either spray a 12-cup muffin pan with nonstick spray, or line with paper liners.
2. In a medium bowl whisk together the bananas, buttermilk, butter, egg, and vanilla. Set aside.
3. In a large bowl add the flour, sugar, cinnamon, baking soda, baking powder, and salt. Whisk until well combined.
4. Make a well in the center of the dry ingredients and pour in the wet ingredients. With a wooden spoon or spatula, gently fold the mixture until just combined, about 10 strokes. Do not overmix. Add the cranberries and white chocolate and fold to mix, about 2–3 strokes.
5. Divide the batter evenly between the prepared muffin cups and bake for 18–20 minutes, or until the muffins spring back when gently pressed in the center and the tops are golden brown. Cool in the pan for 3 minutes, then remove the muffins from the pan to a wire rack to cool. Serve warm.

Lime Sesame Muffins

With their pleasing chewy texture and a mild flavor, sesame seeds are a wonderfully diverse ingredient. When the seeds are toasted the flavor transforms from mild to deeply nutty. Here, whole sesame seeds and toasted sesame oil are combined to provide the maximum sesame flavor. A little lime is added to give each bite a spark of freshness!

Yields 18 Muffins

2 cups all-purpose flour

1¼ teaspoons baking powder

½ teaspoon baking soda

½ teaspoon salt

¾ cup sugar

⅓ cup butter, melted and cooled

1 tablespoon toasted sesame oil

1 teaspoon vanilla

1 tablespoon freshly grated lime zest

¾ cup buttermilk

2 eggs

2 tablespoons sesame seeds

1. Preheat oven to 350°F and prepare 18 muffin cups with nonstick spray, or line with paper liners.
2. In a large bowl sift together the flour, baking powder, baking soda, and salt. Once sifted, whisk in the sugar until evenly mixed.
3. In a separate bowl add the melted butter, sesame oil, vanilla, lime zest, buttermilk, and eggs. Whisk until the mixture is well combined.
4. Make a well in the center of the dry ingredients and pour in the wet ingredients. With a wooden spoon or spatula, gently fold the mixture until just combined, about 10–12 strokes. Do not overmix.
5. Divide the batter evenly between the prepared muffin cups and top each with the sesame seeds. Bake for 18–20 minutes, or until the muffins spring back when gently pressed in the center and the tops are golden brown. Cool in the pan for 3 minutes, then remove the muffins from the pan to a wire rack to cool to room temperature.

PART 2
Savory Sensations

Sometimes only something savory will do.

Take a trip to Tuscany with a muffin flavored with pungent rosemary and fruity olive oil, or try an updated spin on a comfort-food classic by making meatloaf muffins stuffed with little balls of marinated mozzarella cheese. Any way you choose to make them, savory muffins are sure to please, and they are sure to impress! Aside from their versatility they have an advantage of being just as easy to prepare as sweet muffins, so making a meal for unexpected guests or preparing a dinner on a busy night is a snap! And with recipes filled with gourmet flavors—such as artichoke, homemade sausage, and tangy feta—your muffins will be delicious and impressive.

So get ready to discover some savory sensations. With muffins this good you may never go back to yeast rolls!

CHAPTER 3

Brunch, Lunch, and Dinner Muffins

When most people think of savory muffins they immediately think of the humble corn muffin. But just as there are limitless varieties of sweet muffins, there are unlimited muffins with a savory edge—and they are just as quick, easy, and gourmet as their sweet counterparts! From hot serrano chiles and creamy smoked cheddar cheese to more unique additions such as fresh crab and sun-dried tomatoes, today's savory ingredients can turn even the most basic muffin into a spectacular upscale treat bursting with flavor!

In addition to being delicious, today's savory muffins are also versatile; they not only make a great addition to most any meal, but they can even be a meal in themselves. From juicy meatloaf muffins stuffed with melting mozzarella cheese, to muffins with all the spicy flavors of Tex-Mex casseroles, these brunch, lunch, and dinner muffins can be served as appetizers, as a main dish, or for almost any course in between. Enjoy!

Bell Pepper and Cheddar Corn Muffins

Red bell peppers have a vibrant red color and a lovely, sweet flavor. In this recipe bell peppers are combined with sharp Cheddar cheese to recreate, in muffin form, the classic Southern dish, pimento cheese. These muffins are festive and the perfect thing to serve with fried chicken or fried eggs. If you want to give these muffins a slightly smoky flavor, simply roast the peppers on the grill before adding them to the batter.

Yields 18 Muffins

1 cup cornmeal

1 cup all-purpose flour

1 tablespoon white sugar

1½ teaspoons baking powder

¼ teaspoon baking soda

½ teaspoon salt

2 eggs

¼ cup butter, melted and cooled

1 cup buttermilk

1 red bell pepper, cored and finely chopped

1 cup coarsely shredded sharp Cheddar cheese

1. Preheat oven to 350°F and prepare 18 muffin cups with nonstick spray, or line with paper liners.
2. In a large bowl whisk together the cornmeal, flour, sugar, baking powder, baking soda, and salt until well mixed.
3. In a medium bowl add the eggs, butter, and buttermilk, and whisk until evenly combined.
4. Make a well in the center of the dry ingredients and pour in the wet ingredients. With a wooden spoon or spatula, gently fold the mixture until just combined, about 10 strokes. Do not overmix. Add the diced pepper and cheese and fold to evenly distribute, about 3 strokes.
5. Divide the batter evenly between the prepared muffin cups. Bake for 18–20 minutes, or until the muffins spring back when gently pressed in the center and the tops are golden brown. If the tops are too pale, place the muffins under the broiler for 1–2 minutes to give them some color. Cool in the pan for 3 minutes, then remove the muffins from the pan to cool on a wire rack. Enjoy warm.

Garlic Chive Buttermilk Muffins

Fresh chives have a mild, pleasing onion flavor that deserves to shine. In this tender muffin, the subtle tang of buttermilk pairs beautifully with the freshness of the chives. The buttermilk also helps keep these muffins light and wonderfully moist. These fluffy muffins are superb as an accompaniment to potato soup.

Yields 18 Muffins

1 clove garlic, minced

2 teaspoons butter

2 cups all-purpose flour

1½ teaspoons baking powder

¼ teaspoon baking soda

½ teaspoon salt

2 eggs

⅓ cup butter, melted and cooled

2 tablespoons cream cheese, at room temperature

1 cup buttermilk

2 tablespoons freshly chopped chives

Garlic-Infused Butter, optional (see Chapter 5)

1. In a small sauté pan add the garlic and butter, and cook over medium heat until the garlic is fragrant and soft, about 1 minute. Remove from the heat and cool to room temperature.
2. Heat oven to 350°F and prepare 18 muffin cups with nonstick spray, or line with paper liners.
3. In a large bowl whisk together the flour, baking powder, baking soda, and salt until well combined.
4. In a medium bowl add the garlic, eggs, butter, cream cheese, buttermilk, and chives. Whisk until evenly mixed.
5. Make a well in the center of the dry ingredients and pour in the wet ingredients. With a wooden spoon or spatula, gently fold the mixture until just combined, about 10–12 strokes. Do not overmix.
6. Divide the batter evenly between the prepared muffin cups. Bake for 18–20 minutes, or until the muffins spring back when gently pressed in the center and the tops are golden brown. If the tops are too pale, place the muffins under the broiler for 1–2 minutes to give them some color. Cool in the pan for 3 minutes, then remove the muffins from the pan to a wire rack to cool. Enjoy warm with Garlic-Infused Butter, if desired.

Ham and Swiss Muffins

Pungent and nutty, rich Swiss cheese is traditionally paired with smoky ham. For this recipe the ham is cooked until it is slightly browned, which brings out even more of its meaty flavor. These elegant muffins are good any time of day, but if you'd like to serve them as an appetizer, make them in mini-muffin pans (which will give you about 40 mini-muffins) to get your gathering off to a tasty start!

Yields 18 Muffins

2 tablespoons butter

1 cup chopped ham

2 cups all-purpose flour

1½ teaspoons baking powder

¼ teaspoon baking soda

½ teaspoon salt

¼ teaspoon nutmeg

2 eggs

1 tablespoon honey

⅓ cup butter, melted and cooled

1 cup whole milk

1 cup shredded Swiss cheese

1. In a medium skillet, warm the butter over medium heat until it foams. Add the ham and cook, stirring frequently, until it has browned slightly, about 8 minutes. Remove the pan from the heat and allow to cool to room temperature.

2. Preheat oven to 350°F and prepare 18 muffin cups with nonstick spray, or line with paper liners.

3. In a large bowl whisk together the flour, baking powder, baking soda, salt, and nutmeg until well combined.

4. In a medium bowl add the eggs, honey, butter, and milk. Whisk until evenly mixed.

5. Make a well in the center of the dry ingredients and pour in the wet ingredients. With a wooden spoon or spatula, gently fold the mixture until just combined, about 10 strokes. Do not overmix. Add the ham and Swiss cheese and fold to mix, about 2–3 strokes.

6. Divide the batter evenly between the prepared muffin cups. Bake for 18–20 minutes, or until the muffins spring back when gently pressed in the center and the tops are golden brown. If the tops are too pale, place the muffins under the broiler for 1–2 minutes to give them some color. Cool in the pan for 3 minutes, then remove the muffins from the pan to a wire rack to cool. Enjoy warm.

Herbed Cornbread Stuffing Muffins

This recipe takes a Thanksgiving favorite, cornbread stuffing, and transforms it into individual muffins for easy sharing. The blend of fresh herbs is what really elevates this baked goodness into something special. If fresh herbs are not available in your store, use half the amount of dry herbs since they have a more concentrated flavor. For a little bit of zing and a little sweetness, consider folding ½ cup of either dried cranberries or cherries into these muffins.

Yields 24 Muffins

¾ cup all-purpose flour

¾ cup yellow cornmeal

2 tablespoons sugar

1½ teaspoons baking powder

1½ teaspoons salt, divided use

6 eggs, beaten, divided use

1 cup buttermilk

⅓ cup butter, melted and cooled

½ cup butter

1 rib celery, chopped fine

1 large onion, chopped fine

1 teaspoon pepper

1 tablespoon chopped fresh parsley

2 teaspoons chopped fresh sage

1 teaspoon chopped fresh thyme

1 teaspoon chopped rosemary

1 Fuji apple, peeled, cored and grated

10 slices oven-dried white bread, crumbled

6 cups chicken stock

1. Preheat oven to 350°F and spray an 8-inch square baking pan and 24 muffin cups with nonstick cooking spray.
2. In a medium bowl combine the flour, cornmeal, sugar, baking powder, and ½ teaspoon of the salt. Whisk to combine.
3. In a separate bowl combine 1 of the beaten eggs, the buttermilk, and the ⅓ cup melted butter. Whisk until smooth, then pour the wet ingredients into the dry. Mix until the dry ingredients are just moistened, then transfer the mixture to the prepared pan. Bake for 20–25 minutes, or until the cornbread is puffed, golden brown, and springs back when gently pressed in the center.
4. Allow the cornbread to cool to room temperature, then cut the cornbread into ½-inch cubes.
5. In a large skillet over medium heat add the butter. Once the butter foams, add the celery, onion, remaining teaspoon of salt, pepper, parsley, sage, thyme, and rosemary. Cook until the celery and onions have softened, about 10 minutes.
6. In a large bowl combine the cubed cornbread, grated apple, and crumbled white bread. Pour over the sautéed vegetable mixture and toss to mix. Add the chicken stock and remaining 5 beaten eggs and stir to mix. This mixture will be very wet.
7. Divide the mixture between the prepared muffin cups and bake for 25–30 minutes, or until the muffins are golden brown and reach an internal temperature of 160°F. Cool the muffins for 10 minutes before serving. Enjoy warm.

Goat Cheese and Leek Muffins

Goat Cheese and Leek Muffins

Goat cheese has a mild, tangy flavor that goes well with the mild, almost sweet flavor of leeks. Sautéing the leeks in butter helps to bring out their natural sugar, and softens their somewhat sharp onion flavor to ensure that it balances well with the goat cheese. If you don't care for goat cheese you can substitute cream cheese or mascarpone cheese instead.

Yields 18 Muffins

2 tablespoons butter

1 leek, halved, washed, dried, and finely chopped

2 cups all-purpose flour

1½ teaspoons baking powder

¼ teaspoon baking soda

½ teaspoon salt

2 eggs

1 tablespoon honey

¼ cup butter, melted and cooled

¼ cup goat cheese, at room temperature

1 cup buttermilk

1. In a medium skillet, heat the butter over medium heat until it foams. Add the leeks and cook, stirring frequently, until they soften, about 8 minutes. Remove the pan from the heat and allow to cool to room temperature.
2. Preheat oven to 350°F and prepare 18 muffin cups with nonstick spray, or line with paper liners.
3. In a large bowl whisk together the flour, baking powder, baking soda, and salt until well combined.
4. In a medium bowl add the cooled leeks, eggs, honey, butter, goat cheese, and buttermilk. Whisk until evenly mixed.
5. Make a well in the center of the dry ingredients and pour in the wet ingredients. With a wooden spoon or spatula, gently fold the mixture until just combined, about 10–12 strokes. Do not overmix.
6. Divide the batter evenly between the prepared muffin cups. Bake for 18–20 minutes, or until the muffins spring back when gently pressed in the center and the tops are golden brown. If the tops are too pale, place the muffins under the broiler for 1–2 minutes to give them some color. Cool in the pan for 3 minutes, then remove the muffins from the pan to a wire rack to cool. Enjoy warm.

Huevos Rancheros Muffins

Huevos rancheros, or ranch-style eggs, is a hearty dish of corn tortillas, spicy tomato sauce, and a fried egg. This muffin uses all the flavors of the original but presents it in a stunning new way. Here the base of the muffins is a corn tortilla, salsa, egg, and cheese mixture that is then topped with an egg and baked until the egg is just set. It makes an excellent—and impressive—addition to a brunch or lunch menu.

Yields 6 Muffins

2 tablespoons butter

1 medium onion, chopped

1 jalapeño, chopped

1 clove garlic, minced

8 eggs, divided use

½ cup tomato salsa

½ teaspoon salt

1 cup whole milk

1 tablespoon all-purpose flour

8 corn tortillas, cut into 1-inch pieces

1½ cups shredded Cheddar cheese

1. In a medium skillet warm the butter over medium heat until it foams. Add the onion and jalapeño and cook, stirring frequently, until softened, about 8 minutes. Add the garlic and cook until fragrant, about 1 minute. Remove the pan from the heat and allow to cool to room temperature.
2. Preheat oven to 350°F and prepare 6 large (Texas size) muffin cups with nonstick spray.
3. In a large bowl whisk together 2 of the eggs, the salsa, salt, milk, and flour until well combined.
4. Divide half the tortilla strips among the prepared muffin cups. Divide 1 cup of the cheese over the tortillas and top with the remaining tortilla strips. Pour the liquid mixture evenly over the tortillas, then crack one egg on top of each muffin. Sprinkle the tops of the eggs with the remaining cheese.
5. Bake for 25–30 minutes, or until the egg whites are set and the yolk is still slightly loose. Cool in the pan for 5 minutes, then carefully remove the muffins from the pan. Enjoy hot.

Loaded Baked Potato Muffins

These delicious muffins have bits of real potato baked right inside along with traditional toppings such as shredded cheese, chives, and bits of crisply cooked bacon. They're an amazing addition to brunch, lunch, or dinner, and are best when served slightly warm, when the flavors of the cheese and bacon are more pronounced.

Yields 12 Muffins

1 medium russet potato

1¼ cups all-purpose flour

1 teaspoon baking powder

¼ teaspoon baking soda

¼ teaspoon salt

⅓ cup butter, melted and cooled

¼ cup buttermilk

¼ cup sour cream

1 egg

4 strips bacon, cooked crisp and chopped

2 tablespoons chopped fresh chives

½ cup shredded sharp Cheddar cheese

1. Preheat oven to 350°F and either spray a 12-cup muffin pan with nonstick spray or line with paper liners.
2. Prick the potato with a fork on both sides. Place the potato directly on the rack of the oven and bake for 1 hour or until a fork inserted into the potato slides in easily. Cool to room temperature, and peel away the skin and discard. Roughly mash the potato.
3. In a large bowl sift together the flour, baking powder, baking soda, and salt.
4. In a separate bowl whisk together the butter, buttermilk, sour cream, and egg until well combined. Stir in the potato.
5. Make a well in the center of the dry ingredients and pour in the wet ingredients. With a wooden spoon or spatula, gently fold the mixture until just combined, about 10 strokes. Do not overmix. Add the bacon, chives, and cheese, and fold to mix, about 2–3 strokes.
6. Divide the batter evenly between the prepared muffin cups. Bake for 18–20 minutes, or until the muffins spring back when gently pressed in the center and the tops are golden brown. If the tops are too pale, place the muffins under the broiler for 1–2 minutes to give them some color. Cool in the pan for 3 minutes, then remove the muffins from the pan to a wire rack to cool. Enjoy warm.

Queso Blanco Corn Muffins

Queso blanco is a delicious, creamy white cheese dip served in Tex-Mex restaurants throughout the Southwest. This highly addictive dip is flavored with sautéed onions, garlic, and spicy peppers like jalapeños and serranos that are then blended with mild white cheeses. The surprisingly creamy texture and the flavor of queso blanco baked into a muffin is sure to be a hit wherever these are served!

Yields 18 Muffins

1 tablespoon butter

½ medium onions, finely chopped

1 serrano pepper, finely chopped

1 clove garlic, minced

1 cup white cornmeal

1 cup all-purpose flour

1½ teaspoons baking powder

¼ teaspoon baking soda

½ teaspoon salt

2 eggs

⅓ cup butter, melted and cooled

1 cup half-and-half

1¼ cups shredded queso quesadilla
   or white American cheese

Garlic Chile Cream Cheese Spread,
   optional (see Chapter 5)

1. In a medium skillet warm the butter over medium heat until it foams. Add the onion and serrano and cook, stirring frequently, until softened, about 8 minutes. Add the garlic and cook until fragrant, about 1 minute. Remove the pan from the heat and allow to cool to room temperature.
2. Preheat oven to 350°F and prepare 18 muffin cups with nonstick spray, or line with paper liners.
3. In a large bowl whisk together the cornmeal, flour, baking powder, baking soda, and salt until well mixed.
4. In a medium bowl add the eggs, butter, and half-and-half, and whisk until evenly combined.
5. Make a well in the center of the dry ingredients and pour in the wet ingredients. With a wooden spoon or spatula, gently fold the mixture until just combined, about 10 strokes. Do not overmix. Add the onion mixture and cheese, and fold to evenly distribute, about 3 strokes.
6. Divide the batter evenly between the prepared muffin cups. Bake for 18–20 minutes, or until the muffins spring back when gently pressed in the center and the tops are golden brown. If the tops are too pale, place the muffins under the broiler for 1–2 minutes to give them some color. Cool in the pan for 3 minutes, then remove the muffins from the pan to cool on a wire rack. Enjoy these muffins warm with a little Garlic Chile Cream Cheese Spread, if desired.

Sausage and Cranberry Stuffing Muffins

Savory and just a little sweet, these muffins make a wonderful addition to a meal of roasted turkey or chicken. The sausage keeps this stuffing very moist, and since the sausage is already seasoned it adds a lot of flavor. Dried cranberries, which keep this muffin from being too savory, plump up as they bake, which means they are tender and not the least bit chewy.

Yields 20 Muffins

½ pound sweet Italian sausage

½ cup butter

2 ribs celery, chopped fine

1 large onion, chopped fine

1 teaspoon salt

1 teaspoon pepper

1 teaspoon poultry seasoning

1 Granny Smith apple, peeled, cored and grated

3 cups chicken stock

3 eggs, beaten

1 cup dried cranberries

10 cups cubed sourdough bread, dried overnight

1. Preheat oven to 350°F and prepare 12 muffin cups with nonstick cooking spray.
2. In a large skillet over medium heat add the sausage. Cook, breaking into small pieces, until evenly browned, about 12 minutes. Remove the sausage from the pan and add the butter. Once the butter foams, add the celery, onion, salt, pepper, and poultry seasoning, and cook until the celery and onions have softened, about 10 minutes.
3. In a large bowl combine the sausage, vegetable mix, and apple. Add the chicken stock and beaten eggs and stir to mix. Fold in the cranberries and bread and mix well. Cover with plastic wrap and refrigerate for at least 1 hour so the bread can soak up the egg mixture. This mixture will be very wet.
4. Once chilled, divide the mixture between the prepared muffin cups and bake for 25–30 minutes, or until the muffins are golden brown and reach an internal temperature of 160°F. Cool the muffins for 10 minutes before serving. Enjoy warm.

Rosemary Olive Oil Muffins

Fresh rosemary is quite pungent and is very popular in Italian cooking. Here, along with fruity olive oil, rosemary is the star ingredient in this recipe for a muffin that is moist, savory, and very hard to resist. As dry rosemary does not have the sharpness of fresh rosemary, fresh herbs are really the key to getting the best flavor for this muffin. This decadent muffin is the perfect accompaniment to pasta or as an appetizer served with some salty Italian meats and cheeses.

Yields 18 Muffins

1¾ cups all-purpose flour

¼ cup cornmeal

1½ teaspoons baking powder

¼ teaspoon baking soda

½ teaspoon salt

2 eggs

⅓ cup extra-virgin olive oil

1 cup whole milk

2 tablespoons fresh rosemary, chopped

Compound Herb Butter, optional (see Chapter 5)

1. Preheat oven to 350°F and prepare 18 muffin cups with nonstick spray, or line with paper liners.
2. In a large bowl whisk together the flour, cornmeal, baking powder, baking soda, and salt until well combined.
3. In a medium bowl add the eggs, olive oil, milk, and rosemary. Whisk until evenly mixed.
4. Make a well in the center of the dry ingredients and pour in the wet ingredients. With a wooden spoon or spatula, gently fold the mixture until just combined, about 10–12 strokes. Do not overmix.
5. Divide the batter evenly between the prepared muffin cups. Bake for 18–20 minutes, or until the muffins spring back when gently pressed in the center and the tops are golden brown. If the tops are too pale, place the muffins under the broiler for 1–2 minutes to give them some color. Cool in the pan for 3 minutes, then remove the muffins from the pan to a wire rack to cool. Enjoy warm with a little Compound Herb Butter, if desired.

Sharp Cheddar Ale Muffins

Welsh rarebit is a scrumptious dish consisting of cheese sauce that is baked over the top of hearty bread. While there are many ways to make this dish, the most popular in British and American pubs uses a hoppy ale as the base for the cheese sauce along with mustard and other spices. This recipe uses all the flavors of the popular pub dish but wraps them up into a delicious muffin. These taste best when they are served warm.

Yields 18 Muffins

2 cups all-purpose flour

1½ teaspoons baking powder

¼ teaspoon baking soda

½ teaspoon salt

½ teaspoon dry mustard powder

¼ teaspoon cayenne pepper

2 eggs

⅓ cup butter, melted and cooled

1 cup ale-style beer

2 cups shredded sharp Cheddar cheese

1. Preheat oven to 350°F and prepare 18 muffin cups with nonstick spray, or line with paper liners.
2. In a large bowl whisk together the flour, baking powder, baking soda, salt, mustard powder, and cayenne pepper until well combined.
3. In a medium bowl add the eggs, butter, and beer. Whisk until evenly mixed.
4. Make a well in the center of the dry ingredients and pour in the wet ingredients. With a wooden spoon or spatula, gently fold the mixture until just combined, about 10 strokes. Do not overmix. Add 1½ cups of the shredded cheese and fold to mix, about 2–3 strokes.
5. Divide the batter evenly between the prepared muffin cups and top with the remaining cheese. Bake for 18–20 minutes, or until the muffins spring back when gently pressed in the center and the tops are golden brown. If the tops are too pale, place the muffins under the broiler for 1–2 minutes to give them some color. Cool in the pan for 3 minutes, then remove the muffins from the pan to a wire rack to cool. Enjoy warm.

Quiche Lorraine Muffins

Quiche Lorraine is traditionally a cheesy quiche flavored with smoky bacon. This muffin is basically a handheld version of the original, which makes it perfect for a casual brunch or breakfast on the run. Use a good quality bacon here as it plays such a prominent role in this dish. If you prefer you can use Gruyère or even Swiss cheese instead of Cheddar, or a blend of the two.

Yields 16 Muffins

1 tablespoon butter

1 small onion, chopped

1 clove garlic, minced

½ teaspoon salt

¼ teaspoon white pepper

6 eggs

⅓ cup heavy cream

3 tablespoons all-purpose flour

⅛ teaspoon nutmeg

4 dashes hot sauce, or to taste

12 strips thick-cut bacon, cooked crisp and chopped

2 cups shredded Cheddar cheese

Chopped fresh parsley, optional garnish

1. In a medium skillet, warm the butter over medium heat until it foams. Add the onion and cook until tender, about 5 minutes. Add the garlic and cook until fragrant, about 1 minute. Season with the salt and pepper. Remove the pan from the heat and cool to room temperature.

2. Preheat oven to 350°F and either spray a 12-cup muffin pan with nonstick spray or line with paper liners.

3. In a medium bowl combine the eggs, heavy cream, flour, nutmeg, and hot sauce, and whisk to combine.

4. Divide the sautéed onion, bacon, and cheese among the prepared muffin cups. Pour the egg mixture over the top. Bake for 20–25 minutes, or until the muffins are puffed all over and golden brown on top. Cool for 5 minutes before carefully removing from the pan. If desired, garnish with chopped parsley and serve warm or at room temperature.

Quiche Lorraine Muffins

Smoked Cheddar Jalapeño Corn Muffins

The smoked Cheddar found in this recipe hits a variety of sharp, creamy, and smoky notes, which, when added to this corn muffin, make for a surprisingly decadent experience. The spice of the jalapeño keeps the cheese from being too rich while adding a definite heat and fruity flavor. This Tex-Mex–inspired muffin is sure to spice up any gathering!

Yields 18 Muffins

1 tablespoon butter

1 jalapeño, minced

1 cup cornmeal

1 cup all-purpose flour

1 teaspoon white sugar

1½ teaspoons baking powder

¼ teaspoon baking soda

½ teaspoon salt

½ teaspoon smoked paprika

2 eggs

¼ cup butter, melted and cooled

1 cup buttermilk

1 cup shredded smoked Cheddar cheese

Jalapeño Cheddar Spread, optional (see Chapter 5)

1. In a small skillet warm the butter over medium heat until it foams. Add the jalapeño and cook, stirring often, until softened, about 3 minutes. Remove from the heat and allow to cool.

2. Preheat oven to 350°F and prepare 18 muffin cups with nonstick spray, or line with paper liners.

3. In a large bowl whisk together the cornmeal, flour, sugar, baking powder, baking soda, salt, and smoked paprika until well mixed.

4. In a medium bowl add the cooked jalapeños, eggs, butter, and buttermilk, and whisk until evenly combined.

5. Make a well in the center of the dry ingredients and pour in the wet ingredients. With a wooden spoon or spatula, gently fold the mixture until just combined, about 10 strokes. Do not overmix. Add the cheese and fold to evenly distribute, about 3 strokes.

6. Divide the batter evenly between the prepared muffin cups. Bake for 18–20 minutes, or until the muffins spring back when gently pressed in the center and the tops are golden brown. If the tops are too pale, place the muffins under the broiler for 1–2 minutes to give them some color. Cool in the pan for 3 minutes, then remove the muffins from the pan to cool on a wire rack. Enjoy warm with Jalapeño Cheddar Spread, if desired.

Spicy Sausage and Cheddar Muffins

This recipe makes a perfect breakfast, and can be made in advance and frozen to make your morning easy. Why wouldn't you want to start your day with a muffin filled with chunks of fresh, homemade, maple-flavored sausage?

Yields 18 Muffins

2 strips thick-cut, smoked bacon, cut into 2-inch pieces

¼ pound lean ground pork

2 teaspoons maple syrup

¼ teaspoon fresh sage, finely chopped

¼ teaspoon fresh thyme, finely chopped

⅛ teaspoon fresh rosemary, finely chopped

¼ teaspoon smoked paprika

¼ teaspoon crushed red-pepper flakes

¼ teaspoon salt

¼ teaspoon fresh cracked black pepper

¼ cup cornmeal

1¾ cups all-purpose flour

1 teaspoon white sugar

1½ teaspoons baking powder

¼ teaspoon baking soda

½ teaspoon salt

½ teaspoon smoked paprika

2 eggs

⅓ cup butter, melted and cooled

1 cup buttermilk

1 cup shredded mild Cheddar cheese

1. In the work bowl of a food processor, add the bacon strips and pulse until they are roughly ground, about 10 pulses. Add the ground pork, maple syrup, sage, thyme, rosemary, smoked paprika, red-pepper flakes, salt, and black pepper, and pulse until well combined and smooth, about 15–20 pulses.

2. In a medium skillet over medium heat, add the sausage mixture. Break up the sausage into small pieces, about the size of hazelnuts, and cook until well browned, about 15 minutes. Remove the sausage from the pan and drain well on paper towels.

3. Preheat oven to 350°F and prepare 18 muffin cups with nonstick spray, or line with paper liners.

4. In a large bowl whisk together the cornmeal, flour, sugar, baking powder, baking soda, salt, and smoked paprika until well mixed.

5. In a medium bowl add the eggs, butter, and buttermilk, and whisk until evenly combined.

6. Make a well in the center of the dry ingredients and pour in the wet ingredients. With a wooden spoon or spatula, gently fold the mixture until just combined, about 10 strokes. Do not overmix. Add the sausage and cheese and fold to evenly distribute, about 3 strokes.

7. Divide the batter evenly between the prepared muffin cups. Bake for 18–20 minutes, or until the muffins spring back when gently pressed in the center and the tops are golden brown. If the tops are too pale, place the muffins under the broiler for 1–2 minutes to give them some color. Cool in the pan for 3 minutes, then remove the muffins from the pan to cool on a wire rack. Enjoy warm.

Spinach, Artichoke, and Jalapeño Muffins

Spinach and artichoke are often found in cheesy dips served with corn chips, but in this recipe, these ingredients are baked into a slightly spicy, surprisingly upscale jalapeño muffin! Jalapeño has a fruity flavor that blends exceptionally well with the mild flavor of artichoke. If there are fresh artichokes in season, please feel free to use them here.

Yields 18 Muffins

2 cups all-purpose flour

1 teaspoon white sugar

1¼ teaspoons baking powder

½ teaspoon baking soda

½ teaspoon salt

2 eggs

⅓ cup butter, melted and cooled

½ cup buttermilk

½ cup sour cream

½ cup chopped, frozen spinach, drained well

½ cup jarred artichoke hearts, chopped

1 jalapeño, finely minced

1. Preheat oven to 350°F and prepare 18 muffin cups with nonstick spray, or line with paper liners.
2. In a large bowl whisk together the flour, sugar, baking powder, baking soda, and salt until well mixed.
3. In a medium bowl add the eggs, butter, buttermilk, and sour cream, and whisk until evenly combined.
4. Make a well in the center of the dry ingredients and pour in the wet ingredients. With a wooden spoon or spatula, gently fold the mixture until just combined, about 10 strokes. Do not overmix. Add the spinach, artichoke hearts, and jalapeño, and fold to evenly distribute, about 3 strokes.
5. Divide the batter evenly between the prepared muffin cups. Bake for 18–20 minutes, or until the muffins spring back when gently pressed in the center and the tops are golden brown. If the tops are too pale, place the muffins under the broiler for 1–2 minutes to give them some color. Cool in the pan for 3 minutes, then remove the muffins from the pan to cool on a wire rack. Enjoy warm.

Sun-Dried Tomato and Parmesan Muffins

Sun-dried tomatoes are a staple of Italian cooking. They find their way into gourmet pizzas, salads, and sandwiches, and are even used as a garnish for soups. In this recipe, bits of finely minced sun-dried tomato are folded into a tender Parmesan batter. Brushed with garlic butter once, it bakes to create a super savory—and extremely classy—muffin that's perfect served with brunch, lunch, or dinner.

Yields 18 Muffins

2 tablespoons butter

1 clove garlic, minced

2 cups all-purpose flour

1½ teaspoons baking powder

¼ teaspoon baking soda

½ teaspoon salt

½ teaspoon dry oregano

2 eggs

⅓ cup butter, melted and cooled

1 cup buttermilk

½ cup freshly grated Parmesan cheese

¼ cup finely chopped sun-dried tomatoes

1. In a small sauté pan over medium-low heat, add the butter and warm until it is melted. Add the garlic and slowly cook until it is fragrant and soft, about 3 minutes. Do not let the garlic sizzle or brown. Remove from the heat and set aside.
2. Preheat oven to 350°F and prepare 18 muffin cups with nonstick spray, or line with paper liners.
3. In a large bowl whisk together the flour, baking powder, baking soda, salt, and oregano until well combined.
4. In a medium bowl add the eggs, butter, buttermilk, and Parmesan cheese. Whisk until evenly mixed.
5. Make a well in the center of the dry ingredients and pour in the wet ingredients. With a wooden spoon or spatula, gently fold the mixture until just combined, about 10 strokes. Do not overmix. Add in the sun-dried tomatoes and fold to mix, about 3 strokes.
6. Divide the batter evenly between the prepared muffin cups. Bake for 18–20 minutes, or until the muffins spring back when gently pressed in the center and the tops are golden brown. If the tops are too pale, place the muffins under the broiler for 1–2 minutes to give them some color. While still hot, brush the top of each muffin with the garlic butter. Cool in the pan for 3 minutes, then remove the muffins from the pan to a wire rack to cool. Enjoy warm.

Spiced Pimento Cheese Muffins

Spiced Pimento Cheese Muffins

Pimento cheese is a staple of the South where it is typically served as a spread on crackers or fresh vegetables. Here the flavors of pimento cheese—sharp Cheddar, sweet pimentos, and sumptuous mayonnaise—are incorporated into a delightfully savory muffin. A pinch of cayenne pepper is also added to give a little spicy kick, but if you prefer you can leave this ingredient out.

Yields 18 Muffins

¼ cup cornmeal

1¾ cups all-purpose flour

1 teaspoon white sugar

1¼ teaspoons baking powder

½ teaspoon baking soda

½ teaspoon salt

½ teaspoon cayenne pepper

2 eggs

¼ cup butter, melted and cooled

⅓ cup buttermilk

⅔ cup mayonnaise

1 cup shredded sharp Cheddar cheese

¼ cup drained, diced pimentos

Pimento Cheese Spread, optional (see Chapter 5)

1. Preheat oven to 350°F and prepare 18 muffin cups with nonstick spray, or line with paper liners.
2. In a large bowl whisk together the cornmeal, flour, sugar, baking powder, baking soda, salt, and cayenne pepper until well mixed.
3. In a medium bowl add the eggs, butter, buttermilk, and mayonnaise, and whisk until evenly combined.
4. Make a well in the center of the dry ingredients and pour in the wet ingredients. With a wooden spoon or spatula, gently fold the mixture until just combined, about 10 strokes. Do not overmix. Add the cheese and pimentos and fold to evenly distribute, about 3 strokes.
5. Divide the batter evenly between the prepared muffin cups. Bake for 18–20 minutes, or until the muffins spring back when gently pressed in the center and the tops are golden brown. If the tops are too pale, place the muffins under the broiler for 1–2 minutes to give them some color. Cool in the pan for 3 minutes, then remove the muffins from the pan to cool on a wire rack. Serve with Pimento Cheese Spread, if desired. Enjoy warm or at room temperature.

Caramelized Onion and Bacon Muffins

Caramelized onions have a beautiful golden color and a naturally sweet flavor that perfectly complements the salty, smoky flavor of bacon. Here the two are combined to create a muffin that strikes just the right savory balance of flavor without being overpowering. Topping these muffins is a unique succulent crumble that adds a little smoky flavor and a bright pop of color.

Yields 18 Muffins

1 tablespoon olive oil

1 tablespoon butter

1 medium yellow onion, peeled, thinly sliced

½ teaspoon sugar

2 cups all-purpose flour

1½ teaspoons baking powder

¼ teaspoon baking soda

½ teaspoon salt

2 eggs

⅓ cup butter, melted and cooled

1 cup buttermilk

5 strips thick-cut bacon, cooked crisp and crumbled

1 recipe Savory Smoked Paprika Bacon Crumble (see Chapter 6)

Smoky Bacon Spread, optional (see Chapter 5)

1. In a medium skillet over medium-low heat, warm the olive oil and butter until the butter is melted. Then add the sliced onions and cook slowly until the onions are very soft, about 10 minutes. Do not let the oil sizzle or the onions brown. Add the sugar and cook, stirring occasionally, until the onions are a deep golden brown, about 20 minutes. If the onions get dry or stick to the pan, add a few tablespoons of water. Once cooked, cool to room temperature and then roughly chop. Set aside.

2. Preheat oven to 350°F and prepare 18 muffin cups with nonstick spray, or line with paper liners.

3. In a large bowl whisk together the flour, baking powder, baking soda, and salt until well combined.

4. In a medium bowl add the eggs, butter, and buttermilk. Whisk until evenly mixed.

5. Make a well in the center of the dry ingredients and pour in the wet ingredients. With a wooden spoon or spatula, gently fold the mixture until just combined, about 10 strokes. Do not overmix. Add in the caramelized onions and bacon and fold to mix, about 3 strokes.

6. Divide the batter evenly between the prepared muffin cups and top with the Savory Smoked Paprika Bacon Crumble. Bake for 18–20 minutes, or until the muffins spring back when gently pressed in the center and the tops are golden brown. If the tops are too pale, place the muffins under the broiler for 1–2 minutes to give them some color. Cool in the pan for 3 minutes, then re-move the muffins from the pan to a wire rack to cool. Enjoy these muffins warm with a smear of Smoky Bacon Spread, if desired.

Crab Salad Corn Muffins

Fresh lump crab is prized for its mild, sweet flavor and delicate texture. In this muffin this delicious ingredient is baked into a corn muffin that is reminiscent of a baked crab dip. The secret to making this muffin super flavorful is the seafood seasoning. Usually a blend of spices and herbs enhance the flavor of fish and shellfish but here the seasoning is cooked along with onions, celery, and garlic to mellow the flavors and toast the spices. These muffins are a wonderful seafood delight!

Yields 18 Muffins

1 tablespoon butter
¼ cup finely diced celery
¼ cup finely diced onion
1 clove garlic, minced
½ teaspoon seafood seasoning, such as Old Bay
½ cup cornmeal
1½ cups all-purpose flour
1¼ teaspoons baking powder
½ teaspoon baking soda
½ teaspoon salt
½ teaspoon cayenne pepper
2 eggs
¼ cup butter, melted and cooled
⅓ cup mayonnaise
⅔ cup half-and-half
¼ cup fresh or frozen corn kernels
½ cup lump crab meat
Compound Herb Butter, optional (see Chapter 5)

1. In a small sauté pan, warm the butter over medium heat until it foams. Add the celery and onion and cook until tender, about 5 minutes. Add the garlic and seafood seasoning and cook until the garlic is fragrant, about 3 minutes. Remove from the heat and set aside to cool.
2. Preheat oven to 350°F and prepare 18 muffin cups with nonstick spray, or line with paper liners.
3. In a large bowl whisk together the cornmeal, flour, baking powder, baking soda, salt, and cayenne pepper until well mixed.
4. In a medium bowl add the eggs, butter, mayonnaise, and half-and-half, and whisk until evenly combined.
5. Make a well in the center of the dry ingredients and pour in the wet ingredients. With a wooden spoon or spatula, gently fold the mixture until just combined, about 10 strokes. Do not overmix. Add the onion mixture, corn, and crab meat, and fold to evenly distribute, about 3 strokes.
6. Divide the batter evenly between the prepared muffin cups. Bake for 18–20 minutes, or until the muffins spring back when gently pressed in the center and the tops are golden brown. If the tops are too pale, place the muffins under the broiler for 1–2 minutes to give them some color. Cool in the pan for 3 minutes, then remove the muffins from the pan to cool on a wire rack. Enjoy warm with Compound Herb Butter, if desired.

Cheesy Shrimp Muffins

Shrimp and grits is a popular down-home comfort food that has seen a resurgence in popularity, particularly in gourmet restaurants where the humble dish is elevated with herbs, spices, and cheeses. Here small shrimp, called salad shrimp, are folded into a light corn muffin that is flavored with thyme and smoked Gouda cheese. The muffins' creamy texture comes from the cream cheese that is added to the batter, which makes the texture of these creations similar to that of corn grits.

Yields 18 Muffins

2 tablespoons butter

½ medium onion, finely chopped

¼ teaspoon fresh thyme, chopped

1 clove garlic, minced

1 cup all-purpose flour

1 cup cornmeal

1½ teaspoons baking powder

¼ teaspoon baking soda

½ teaspoon salt

2 eggs

⅓ cup butter, melted and cooled

2 tablespoons cream cheese, at room temperature

1 cup buttermilk

1 cup small salad shrimp, cooked

1 cup shredded smoked Gouda cheese

Smoky Cayenne Butter, optional (see Chapter 5)

1. In a small sauté pan, warm the butter over medium heat until it foams. Add the onion and thyme and cook until the onion is tender, about 5 minutes. Add the garlic and cook until the garlic is fragrant, about 1 minute. Remove from the heat and set aside to cool.

2. Preheat oven to 350°F and prepare 18 muffin cups with nonstick spray, or line with paper liners.

3. In a large bowl whisk together the flour, cornmeal, baking powder, baking soda, and salt until well combined.

4. In a medium bowl add the eggs, butter, cream cheese, and buttermilk. Whisk until evenly mixed.

5. Make a well in the center of the dry ingredients and pour in the wet ingredients. With a wooden spoon or spatula, gently fold the mixture until just combined, about 10 strokes. Do not overmix. Add in the onion mixture, shrimp, and cheese, and fold to mix, about 3 strokes.

6. Divide the batter evenly between the prepared muffin cups. Bake for 18–20 minutes, or until the muffins spring back when gently pressed in the center and the tops are golden brown. If the tops are too pale, place the muffins under the broiler for 1–2 minutes to give them some color. Cool in the pan for 3 minutes, then remove the muffins from the pan to a wire rack to cool. Spread with Smoky Cayenne Butter if desired and enjoy warm.

Mozzarella Stuffed Meatloaf Muffins

These little muffins are not your mother's meatloaf! Made with spicy sausage, ground beef, ground pork, and ground bacon, this is a moist meatloaf that does not require any fillers, like bread crumbs. They are then stuffed with little balls of marinated mozzarella that melt during baking to create a deliciously gooey prize in the center of every muffin. These savory muffins are "glazed" with ketchup, but you could also use barbecue sauce if you prefer.

Yields 8 Muffins

8 strips thick-cut smoked bacon, cut into 2-inch pieces

10 ounces lean ground beef

10 ounces lean ground pork

8 ounces spicy bulk Italian sausage

2 tablespoons butter

1 medium onion, finely chopped

1 rib celery, finely chopped

2 cloves garlic, minced

1 carrot, peeled and finely grated

½ teaspoon fresh thyme

½ teaspoon fresh rosemary, chopped

1 teaspoon smoked paprika

½ teaspoon cayenne pepper

½ teaspoon salt

½ teaspoon fresh cracked black pepper

1 egg, beaten

1 teaspoon Worcestershire sauce

8 small marinated mozzarella balls, about 1 inch in diameter

¼ cup ketchup

1. Preheat oven to 425°F and prepare 8 muffin cups with nonstick spray.
2. In the work bowl of a food processor, add the bacon. Pulse until the bacon is uniformly ground, about 20 pulses.
3. In a large bowl combine the ground bacon, beef, pork, and sausage. Mix lightly to combine. Cover and set aside.
4. In a large skillet, warm the butter over medium heat until it foams. Add the onion and celery and cook until softened, about 5 minutes. Add the garlic and cook until just fragrant, about 1 minute. Allow to cool to room temperature.
5. Add the onion mixture to the ground meat along with the grated carrot, thyme, rosemary, smoked paprika, cayenne pepper, salt, black pepper, egg, and Worcestershire sauce. Mix until evenly combined. Do not overmix.
6. Divide half the mixture evenly on waxed paper. Place a mozzarella ball in the center of each muffin, then top with the remaining meat mixture, and roll to ensure the cheese is completely encased in the meat. Put each large meatball into the prepared muffin cups and brush the tops with ketchup. Bake for 12 minutes, then reduce the heat to 350°F and bake for an additional 15–20 minutes, or until the meat around the edges of the muffins reaches an internal temperature of 160°F and the muffins are golden brown and crusty. Cool for 5 minutes before serving.

Feta and Herb Muffins

Feta is a brined Greek cheese that is popular in Mediterranean dishes such as salads and savory pastries. It can be made from either cow's or goat's milk and it has a tangy, salty flavor that blends well with fresh herbs and olive oil. You can use any Mediterranean herbs you like to flavor this muffin, but this recipe uses chives, parsley, and basil because they have enough flavor to stand up to the chunks of feta.

Yields 18 Muffins

2 cups all-purpose flour

1½ teaspoons baking powder

¼ teaspoon baking soda

½ teaspoon salt

2 eggs

1 tablespoon honey

¼ cup olive oil

¼ cup butter, melted and cooled

1 cup whole milk

1 tablespoon fresh chives, chopped

1 tablespoon fresh Italian parsley, chopped

1 tablespoon fresh basil, chopped

1 cup chopped feta cheese

1. Preheat oven to 350°F and prepare 18 muffin cups with nonstick spray, or line with paper liners.
2. In a large bowl whisk together the flour, baking powder, baking soda, and salt until well combined.
3. In a medium bowl add the eggs, honey, olive oil, butter, milk, chives, Italian parsley, and basil. Whisk until evenly mixed.
4. Make a well in the center of the dry ingredients and pour in the wet ingredients. With a wooden spoon or spatula, gently fold the mixture until just combined, about 10 strokes. Do not overmix. Add the feta cheese and fold to mix, about 2–3 strokes.
5. Divide the batter evenly between the prepared muffin cups. Bake for 18–20 minutes, or until the muffins spring back when gently pressed in the center and the tops are golden brown. If the tops are too pale, place the muffins under the broiler for 1–2 minutes to give them some color. Cool in the pan for 3 minutes then remove the muffins from the pan to a wire rack to cool. Enjoy warm.

Zucchini Cheese Muffins

Zucchini is almost magical when baked into breads due to the loads of moisture it adds and the subtle flavor that is difficult to detect. Typically you find zucchini in sweet breads and cakes, but here it is baked into a cheese muffin that is perfect with a bowl of soup, or with nothing more than a little smear of the Compound Herb Butter from Chapter 5.

Yields 18 Muffins

2 cups all-purpose flour

1½ teaspoons baking powder

¼ teaspoon baking soda

½ teaspoon salt

2 eggs

2 tablespoons honey

½ cup butter, melted and cooled

1 cup buttermilk

½ cup shredded Cheddar cheese

2 cups grated zucchini

Compound Herb Butter, optional
   (see Chapter 5)

1. Preheat oven to 350°F and prepare 18 muffin cups with nonstick spray, or line with paper liners.
2. In a large bowl whisk together the flour, baking powder, baking soda, and salt until well combined.
3. In a medium bowl add the eggs, honey, butter, and buttermilk. Whisk until evenly mixed.
4. Make a well in the center of the dry ingredients and pour in the wet ingredients. With a wooden spoon or spatula, gently fold the mixture until just combined, about 10 strokes. Do not overmix. Add the shredded cheese and zucchini and fold to mix, about 2–3 strokes.
5. Divide the batter evenly between the prepared muffin cups. Bake for 18–20 minutes, or until the muffins spring back when gently pressed in the center and the tops are golden brown. If the tops are too pale, place the muffins under the broiler for 1–2 minutes to give them some color. Cool in the pan for 3 minutes, then remove the muffins from the pan to a wire rack to cool. Enjoy warm with Compound Herb Butter, if desired.

King Ranch Chicken Muffins

King Ranch Chicken is a popular Tex-Mex casserole that originated in South Texas. It is a recipe that replaces the corn tortillas with a hearty corn muffin that has roast chicken, pepper, and cheese folded into the batter. These are a perfect on-the-run meal, but they are also exceptionally good with a cup of soup and a green salad.

Yields 18 Muffins

2 tablespoons butter

½ medium onion, finely chopped

1 serrano chile, minced

¼ cup canned tomatoes with green chiles (Ro*tel brand)

1 clove garlic, minced

1 cup all-purpose flour

1 cup yellow cornmeal

1½ teaspoons baking powder

¼ teaspoon baking soda

½ teaspoon salt

½ teaspoon smoked paprika

¼ teaspoon cayenne pepper

2 eggs

⅓ cup butter, melted and cooled

1 cup buttermilk

1 cup shredded roast chicken breast

1 cup shredded Cheddar jack cheese

1. In a small sauté pan over medium heat, warm the butter until it foams. Add the onion and serrano and cook until tender, about 5 minutes. Add the tomatoes and garlic and cook until the garlic is fragrant, about 3 minutes. Remove from the heat and set aside to cool.

2. Preheat oven to 350°F and prepare 18 muffin cups with nonstick spray, or line with paper liners.

3. In a large bowl whisk together the flour, cornmeal, baking powder, baking soda, salt, smoked paprika, and cayenne pepper until well combined.

4. In a medium bowl add the eggs, butter, and buttermilk. Whisk until evenly mixed.

5. Make a well in the center of the dry ingredients and pour in the wet ingredients. With a wooden spoon or spatula, gently fold the mixture until just combined, about 10 strokes. Do not overmix. Add in the onion mixture, shredded chicken, and cheese, and fold to mix, about 3 strokes.

6. Divide the batter evenly between the prepared muffin cups. Bake for 18–20 minutes, or until the muffins spring back when gently pressed in the center and the tops are golden brown. If the tops are too pale, place the muffins under the broiler for 1–2 minutes to give them some color. Cool in the pan for 3 minutes, then remove the muffins from the pan to a wire rack to cool. Enjoy warm.

King Ranch Chicken Muffins

Ham and Mushroom Muffins

Mushrooms are available in many tasty varieties, both fresh and dried, with different flavors and textures. This recipe calls for two types of fresh mushrooms, the hearty crimini and the floral oyster, which are sautéed with garlic, then combined with diced honey ham and fontina cheese to create a hearty, satisfying muffin. The sweetness of the honey ham adds a lighter note to contrast the savory mushrooms. When baked in a mini-muffin pan, this recipe creates an excellent appetizer that is perfect to serve with cocktails.

Yields 18 Muffins

2 tablespoons butter

1 cup sliced oyster mushrooms

1 cup sliced crimini mushrooms

1 clove garlic, minced

1½ cups all-purpose flour

½ cup cornmeal

1½ teaspoons baking powder

¼ teaspoon baking soda

½ teaspoon salt

2 eggs

½ cup butter, melted and cooled

1 cup buttermilk

1 cup diced honey ham

½ cup shredded fontina cheese

1. In a small sauté pan over medium heat, warm the butter until it foams. Add the mushrooms and cook until they are lightly browned and tender, about 8 minutes. Add the garlic and cook until the garlic is fragrant, about 1 minute. Remove from the heat and set aside to cool.

2. Preheat oven to 350°F and prepare 18 muffin cups with nonstick spray, or line with paper liners.

3. In a large bowl whisk together the flour, cornmeal, baking powder, baking soda, and salt until well combined.

4. In a medium bowl add the eggs, butter, and buttermilk. Whisk until evenly mixed.

5. Make a well in the center of the dry ingredients and pour in the wet ingredients. With a wooden spoon or spatula, gently fold the mixture until just combined, about 10 strokes. Do not overmix. Add in the mushroom mixture, ham, and cheese, and fold to mix, about 3 strokes.

6. Divide the batter evenly between the prepared muffin cups. Bake for 18–20 minutes, or until the muffins spring back when gently pressed in the center and the tops are golden brown. If the tops are too pale, place the muffins under the broiler for 1–2 minutes to give them some color. Cool in the pan for 3 minutes, then remove the muffins from the pan to a wire rack to cool. Enjoy warm.

Ham and Currant Muffins

The currant is a small dried berry, similar to a raisin, but with a sweeter, more floral flavor. Black currants are the main ingredient in *crème de cassis*, and the currant is vastly popular in Europe. The sweet flavor of currants makes a lovely foil to smoky ham, and here the two are added to a muffin that is flavored with sour cream and just a touch of honey. These make a wonderful breakfast, but are just as good with dinner, especially during the holidays!

Yields 18 Muffins

2 cups all-purpose flour

1½ teaspoons baking powder

¼ teaspoon baking soda

½ teaspoon salt

2 eggs

2 tablespoons honey

½ cup butter, melted and cooled

1 cup whole milk

1 cup diced smoked ham

½ cup dried currants

1. Preheat oven to 350°F and prepare 18 muffin cups with nonstick spray, or line with paper liners.
2. In a large bowl whisk together the flour, baking powder, baking soda, and salt until well combined.
3. In a medium bowl add the eggs, honey, butter, and milk. Whisk until evenly mixed.
4. Make a well in the center of the dry ingredients and pour in the wet ingredients. With a wooden spoon or spatula, gently fold the mixture until just combined, about 10 strokes. Do not overmix. Add the ham and currants and fold to mix, about 2–3 strokes.
5. Divide the batter evenly between the prepared muffin cups. Bake for 18–20 minutes, or until the muffins spring back when gently pressed in the center and the tops are golden brown. If the tops are too pale, place the muffins under the broiler for 1–2 minutes to give them some color. Cool in the pan for 3 minutes, then remove the muffins from the pan to a wire rack to cool. Enjoy warm.

Pepperoni Pizza Muffins

Pepperoni pizza is one of the most popular pizza choices going and this cheesy muffin turns these everyday flavors into an extraordinarily sophisticated dish! If you'd like, feel free to add other toppings, like mushrooms, onions, bell peppers, or sliced olives, or other meats like sausage, ham, or hamburger. Serve these muffins on their own or with a side of tomato sauce for dipping if you like it saucy!

Yields 18 Muffins

½ cup chopped pepperoni

2 cups all-purpose flour

1½ teaspoons baking powder

¼ teaspoon baking soda

½ teaspoon oregano

¼ teaspoon thyme

½ teaspoon salt

2 eggs

⅓ cup butter, melted and cooled

1 cup whole milk

½ cup canned diced tomatoes, drained well

1 cup shredded mozzarella cheese

1. In a medium skillet over medium heat, add the pepperoni. Cook until the pepperoni has rendered its fat and is just becoming crisp. Remove the pepperoni from the pan and drain on paper towels.

2. Preheat oven to 350°F and prepare 18 muffin cups with nonstick spray, or line with paper liners.

3. In a large bowl whisk together the flour, baking powder, baking soda, oregano, thyme, and salt until well combined.

4. In a medium bowl add the eggs, butter, and milk. Whisk until evenly mixed.

5. Make a well in the center of the dry ingredients and pour in the wet ingredients. With a wooden spoon or spatula, gently fold the mixture until just combined, about 10 strokes. Do not overmix. Add the pepperoni, tomatoes, and cheese, and fold to mix, about 2–3 strokes.

6. Divide the batter evenly between the prepared muffin cups. Bake for 18–20 minutes, or until the muffins spring back when gently pressed in the center and the tops are golden brown. If the tops are too pale, place the muffins under the broiler for 1–2 minutes to give them some color. Cool in the pan for 3 minutes, then remove the muffins from the pan to a wire rack to cool. Enjoy warm.

CHAPTER 4

Savory, Spicy, and a Little Sweet

In this chapter, exotic flavors, exciting combinations, and unusual ingredients will combine to reveal a whole new world of muffin creations. Fresh strawberries make a lovely ingredient for a muffin, but add in a little diced jalapeño pepper and now you have something brilliant! Coconut muffins are fine on their own, but if you add the crisp, bright flavor of Thai lemongrass you have transformed the perfectly fine into the phenomenal! Thinking outside the box and adding in some exciting twists makes these recipes exceptional. Muffins that combine a little sweet with a little salty or spicy are particularly popular as a part of today's gourmet muffin revolution. To create something exotic you simply need a few exceptional ingredients—some bits of bacon, a splash of salted caramel, or a pinch of spicy peppers—and a little muffin know-how. Striking the right balance is the key because the right balance leads to the best flavor. Knowing just how much spice is right or how much savory will work best with the sweet is easier than you may think! So grab your whisk and get baking because creating exciting muffins with a gourmet edge is easy when you're working with something savory, spicy, and a little sweet!

Maple Bacon Muffins

Pancakes drenched in butter and syrup and served with a side of crispy bacon—what could be better? Well, this same irresistible breakfast is easy to eat—and far less sticky—in muffin form, of course! These beautiful buttery maple muffins are speckled with bits of smoky bacon to recreate the traditional breakfast that is easy to eat on the go. If you like, you could substitute browned breakfast sausage bits for the bacon, or even ham that has been grilled and finely diced.

Yields 18 Muffins

8 strips thick-cut bacon, cooked crisp and chopped

2 cups all-purpose flour

¾ teaspoon baking powder

¾ teaspoon baking soda

½ teaspoon salt

1 cup sugar

⅓ cup butter, melted and cooled

1 teaspoon vanilla

1 cup buttermilk

2 eggs

1. Preheat oven to 350°F and prepare 18 muffin cups with nonstick spray, or line with paper liners.
2. In a large bowl sift together the flour, baking powder, baking soda, and salt. Once sifted, whisk in the sugar until evenly mixed.
3. In a separate bowl add the butter, vanilla, buttermilk, and eggs. Whisk until the mixture is well combined.
4. Make a well in the center of the dry ingredients and pour in the wet ingredients. With a wooden spoon or spatula, gently fold the mixture until just combined, about 10 strokes. Do not overmix. Add the chopped bacon and fold to evenly distribute, about 3 strokes.
5. Divide the batter evenly between the prepared muffin cups. Bake for 18–20 minutes, or until the muffins spring back when gently pressed in the center and the tops are golden brown. Cool in the pan for 3 minutes, then remove the muffins from the pan to cool on a wire rack. Enjoy warm.

Chipotle Swirl Corn Muffins

Chipotle powder packs a lot of smoky flavor and pleasant, but not overpowering, warmth. It is a wonderful addition to a lightly sweet corn muffin, and it's especially nice in this recipe because the chipotle is added in a way that makes a delicate, spicy swirl! These are lovely served with barbecue or steak, but also make a lovely side dish to soup. If you want a muffin that contains the smoky flavor but doesn't have any heat, simply substitute smoked paprika for the chipotle powder.

Yields 18 Muffins

1 cup cornmeal

1 cup all-purpose flour

1½ teaspoons baking powder

¼ teaspoon baking soda

½ teaspoon salt

2 eggs

2 tablespoons honey

½ cup butter, melted and cooled

1 cup buttermilk

2 teaspoons dry chipotle powder

Chorizo Cheddar Cream Cheese, optional (see Chapter 5)

1. Preheat oven to 350°F and prepare 18 muffin cups with nonstick spray, or line with paper liners.
2. In a large bowl whisk together the cornmeal, flour, baking powder, baking soda, and salt until well mixed.
3. In a medium bowl add the eggs, honey, butter, and buttermilk and whisk until evenly combined.
4. Make a well in the center of the dry ingredients and pour in the wet ingredients. With a wooden spoon or spatula, gently fold the mixture until just combined, about 10 strokes. Do not overmix. Pour ⅓ of the batter into a separate bowl and add the chipotle powder. Stir to mix, about 4 strokes.
5. Divide ½ of the plain batter evenly between the prepared muffin cups. Divide the chipotle batter evenly over the plain, then top with the remaining batter. With a butter knife make a figure-eight pattern in each muffin one time. Bake for 18–20 minutes, or until the muffins spring back when gently pressed in the center and the tops are golden brown. If the tops are too pale, place the muffins under the broiler for 1–2 minutes to give them some color. Cool in the pan for 3 minutes, then remove the muffins from the pan to a wire rack to cool to room temperature. Serve with Chorizo Cheddar Cream Cheese, if desired.

Chocolate Chip and Candied Bacon Muffins with Butterscotch Glaze (see Chapter 6)

Chocolate Chip and Candied Bacon Muffins

This muffin is a little eccentric, but in the best possible way! Thick strips of smoked bacon are candied with spiced brown sugar and then added to moist buttermilk chocolate chip muffins to create an unexpected sweet and savory treat. Lovers of sweet and salty bacon treats are guaranteed to love these!

Yields 18 Muffins

9 strips thick-cut bacon

3 tablespoons packed light brown sugar

¼ teaspoon smoked paprika

¼ teaspoon cayenne pepper

¼ teaspoon cinnamon

2 cups all-purpose flour

¾ teaspoon baking powder

¾ teaspoon baking soda

½ teaspoon salt

1 cup packed light brown sugar

⅓ cup canola or vegetable oil

1 teaspoon vanilla

¾ cup buttermilk

2 eggs

1½ cups semisweet chocolate chips

1 tablespoon all-purpose flour

1 recipe Butterscotch Glaze (see Chapter 6)

1. Preheat oven to 350°F and prepare 18 muffin cups with non-stick spray, or line with paper liners.
2. Place the bacon on a baking sheet lined with a metal cooling rack. Bake for 8–10 minutes, or until the bacon begins to render its fat and is light pink in color. In a small bowl combine the 3 tablespoons brown sugar, smoked paprika, cayenne pepper, and cinnamon. Sprinkle the mixture evenly over the bacon and return to the oven for 20–25 minutes, or until the bacon is crisp. Cool to room temperature, then roughly chop the bacon.
3. In a large bowl sift together the flour, baking powder, baking soda, and salt. Once sifted, whisk in the cup of light brown sugar until evenly mixed. In a separate bowl add the oil, vanilla, buttermilk, and eggs. Whisk until the mixture is well combined.
4. Make a well in the center of the dry ingredients and pour in the wet ingredients. With a wooden spoon or spatula, gently fold the mixture until just combined, about 10 strokes. Do not overmix. In a small bowl combine the chocolate chips with the flour until the chips are coated. Pour ¾ of the bacon and the chips into the batter and fold to evenly distribute, about 3 strokes.
5. Divide the batter evenly between the prepared muffin cups. Bake for 18–20 minutes, or until the muffins spring back when gently pressed in the center and the tops are golden brown. Cool in the pan for 3 minutes, then remove the muffins from the pan to cool on a wire rack.
6. Once the muffins have cooled, prepare the Butterscotch Glaze. Dip the tops of the muffins into the warm glaze, allowing the excess to drip off. While the glaze is still wet, sprinkle the reserved bacon over the top. Place the muffins on a cooling rack and allow the glaze to set, about 1 hour, before serving.

Strawberry Jalapeño Muffins

Sweet, ripe strawberries and spicy hot jalapeños have something in common: a surprisingly gourmet, fruity flavor. Here the flavors of jalapeños and strawberries combine to create an unusual, charmingly spicy and sweet muffin! These make a wonderful snack or can be brought along to a picnic as the perfect summertime treat!

Yields 18 Muffins

1 tablespoon butter

1 jalapeño, finely minced

2 cups all-purpose flour

1 teaspoon baking powder

½ teaspoon baking soda

½ teaspoon salt

¾ cup sugar

⅓ cup vegetable or canola oil

¼ cup strawberry preserves, melted and cooled

1 teaspoon vanilla

¾ cup whole milk

2 eggs

2–3 drops red food coloring, optional

1 cup diced fresh strawberries

1. In a medium skillet, warm the butter over medium heat until it foams. Add the jalapeño and cook, stirring frequently, until softened, about 2 minutes. Remove the pan from the heat and allow to cool to room temperature.

2. Preheat oven to 350°F and prepare 18 muffin cups with nonstick spray, or line with paper liners.

3. In a large bowl sift together the flour, baking powder, baking soda, and salt. Once sifted, whisk in the sugar until evenly mixed.

4. In a separate bowl add the oil, strawberry preserves, vanilla, milk, eggs, and red food coloring. Whisk until the mixture is well combined.

5. Make a well in the center of the dry ingredients and pour in the wet ingredients. With a wooden spoon or spatula, gently fold the mixture until just combined, about 10. Do not overmix. Gently fold in the jalapeños and strawberries, about 3 strokes.

6. Divide the batter evenly between the prepared muffin cups. Bake for 18–20 minutes, or until the muffins spring back when gently pressed in the center and the tops are golden brown. Cool in the pan for 3 minutes, then remove the muffins from the pan to a wire rack to cool to room temperature.

Parma Ham and Apricot Muffins

Parma ham, or *prosciutto di Parma,* is a type of dry cured ham originating from the Parma region of Italy. In this recipe, its mild, salty flavor pairs well with the tanginess of the dried apricots. Crisping the ham prior to folding it into the muffins is the key to keeping the bits of ham from being chewy after baking.

Yields 18 Muffins

1 tablespoon butter

1 cup chopped Parma ham

2 cups all-purpose flour

1½ teaspoons baking powder

¼ teaspoon baking soda

½ teaspoon salt

¼ teaspoon nutmeg

2 tablespoons sugar

2 eggs

2 tablespoons honey

⅓ cup butter, melted and cooled

1 cup whole milk

¾ cup diced dried apricots

1. In a medium skillet, warm the butter over medium heat until it foams. Add the Parma ham and cook, stirring frequently, until the ham has crisped, about 8 minutes. Remove the pan from the heat and allow to cool to room temperature.
2. Preheat oven to 350°F and prepare 18 muffin cups with nonstick spray, or line with paper liners.
3. In a large bowl whisk together the flour, baking powder, baking soda, salt, and nutmeg until well combined. Add the sugar and whisk to combine.
4. In a medium bowl add the eggs, honey, butter, and milk. Whisk until evenly mixed.
5. Make a well in the center of the dry ingredients and pour in the wet ingredients. With a wooden spoon or spatula, gently fold the mixture until just combined, about 10 strokes. Do not overmix. Add the Parma ham and apricots and fold to mix, about 2–3 strokes.
6. Divide the batter evenly between the prepared muffin cups. Bake for 18–20 minutes, or until the muffins spring back when gently pressed in the center and the tops are golden brown. If the tops are too pale, place the muffins under the broiler for 1–2 minutes to give them some color. Cool in the pan for 3 minutes, then remove the muffins from the pan to a wire rack to cool. Enjoy warm.

Salted Peanut Crunch Muffins

If you like your muffins to be a little sweet and a little salty, then these will be a dream come true! With their crisp Brown Sugar Streusel topping, crushed salted peanuts, and a drizzle of Salted Caramel Glaze over the top, these muffins take peanuts from low-brow to high-class. They would make a welcome addition to any brunch spread or as a funky addition to a potluck or bake sale! If you prefer, you could use roasted and salted cashews, pecans, or even hazelnuts in place of the peanuts.

Yields 18 Muffins

2 cups all-purpose flour

1 teaspoon baking powder

¾ teaspoon baking soda

½ teaspoon salt

½ teaspoon cinnamon

1 cup packed light brown sugar

⅓ cup butter

1 teaspoon vanilla

½ cup buttermilk

¼ cup peanut butter

2 eggs

1½ cups lightly crushed salted peanuts

1 recipe Brown Sugar Streusel (see Chapter 6)

½ recipe Salted Caramel Glaze (see Chapter 6)

1. Preheat oven to 350°F. Spray a rimmed baking sheet with nonstick cooking spray, and prepare 18 muffin cups with nonstick spray, or line with paper liners.
2. In a large bowl sift together the flour, baking powder, baking soda, salt, and cinnamon. Once sifted, whisk in the brown sugar until evenly mixed.
3. In a separate bowl add the butter, vanilla, buttermilk, peanut butter, and eggs. Whisk until the mixture is well combined.
4. Make a well in the center of the dry ingredients and pour in the wet ingredients. With a wooden spoon or spatula, gently fold the mixture until just combined, about 10 strokes. Do not overmix. Gently fold in 1 cup of the peanuts, about 3 strokes.
5. Divide the batter evenly between the prepared muffin cups, and top with the Brown Sugar Streusel and the remaining ½ cup of peanuts. Bake for 18–20 minutes, or until the muffins spring back when gently pressed in the center and the tops are golden brown. Cool in the pan for 3 minutes, then remove the muffins from the pan to cool to room temperature on a wire rack. Once cooled, drizzle the Salted Caramel Glaze over the muffin tops. Let them stand for 1 hour before serving.

Salted Peanut Crunch Muffins with Brown Sugar Streusel and Salted Caramel Glaze (see Chapter 6)

Sweet Potato Muffins

Sweet potatoes are, as their name implies, naturally sweet and very hearty. When you mix a little puréed sweet potato into things like cakes and muffins, the results are delicious—and perfect for a lovely fall treat! Sweet potato adds an incredible amount of moisture to muffins, and it also extends their life span. If you like, you could add a handful of chopped pecans to this recipe for a nutty twist.

Yields 18 Muffins

1 cup sugar

½ cup butter, melted and cooled

2 eggs, lightly beaten

1 cup sweet potato purée

1¾ cups all-purpose flour

1 teaspoon salt

1 teaspoon baking soda

½ teaspoon baking powder

½ teaspoon cinnamon

¼ teaspoon cardamom

1 tablespoon orange zest

1 cup whole milk

1. Preheat oven to 350°F and prepare 18 muffin cups with nonstick spray, or line with paper liners.
2. In a large bowl combine the sugar and butter. Add the eggs one at a time until they are completely mixed, then stir in the sweet potato. Set aside.
3. In a separate bowl sift together the flour, salt, baking soda, baking powder, cinnamon, cardamom, and orange zest.
4. Add the flour alternately with the milk to the sweet potato mixture, beginning and ending with the flour.
5. Divide the batter evenly between the prepared muffin cups. Bake for 18–20 minutes, or until the muffins spring back when gently pressed in the center and the tops are golden brown. Cool in the pan for 3 minutes, then remove the muffins from the pan to a wire rack to cool to room temperature.

Chocolate Chocolate-Chip Spice Muffins

Nothing sparks the rich, earthy flavor of chocolate better than a pinch of spice! This recipe uses cinnamon, a common partner to chocolate in Latin America, and chipotle powder. The smoky heat of the chipotle powder helps showcase the chocolate, and it gives these muffins a pleasant, warm tingle. These are wonderful for a snow-day snack or as the ending to a spice-infused dinner.

Yields 18 Muffins

1¾ cups all-purpose flour

¼ cup Dutch-processed cocoa powder

¾ teaspoon baking powder

¾ teaspoon baking soda

½ teaspoon salt

¼ teaspoon cinnamon

¼ teaspoon chipotle powder

1 cup packed light brown sugar

⅓ cup canola or vegetable oil

1 teaspoon vanilla

¾ cup buttermilk

2 eggs

1½ cups semisweet chocolate chips

1 tablespoon all-purpose flour

1 recipe Cocoa Streusel (see Chapter 6)

1. Preheat oven to 350°F and prepare 18 muffin cups with nonstick spray, or line with paper liners.
2. In a large bowl sift together the flour, cocoa powder, baking powder, baking soda, salt, cinnamon, and chipotle powder. Once sifted, whisk in the brown sugar until evenly mixed.
3. In a separate bowl add the oil, vanilla, buttermilk, and eggs. Whisk until the mixture is well combined.
4. Make a well in the center of the dry ingredients and pour in the wet ingredients. With a wooden spoon or spatula, gently fold the mixture until just combined, about 10 strokes. Do not overmix. In a small bowl combine the chocolate chips with the flour until the chips are coated. Pour the chips into the batter and fold to evenly distribute, about 3 strokes.
5. Divide the batter evenly between the prepared muffin cups and top with the Cocoa Streusel. Bake for 18–20 minutes, or until the muffins spring back when gently pressed in the center and the tops are golden brown. Cool in the pan for 3 minutes, then remove the muffins from the pan to cool on a wire rack. Enjoy warm.

Apricot 5-Spice Muffins

Chinese 5-spice powder is a unique blend of sweet and savory spices—such as anise, Sichuan peppercorn, and cinnamon—that can be used for sweet and savory cooking. The bold, distinct flavors of this exotic blend are perfect when paired with sweet fruits, such as pears, peaches, and apples. Here, Chinese 5-spice and apricots combine for a spicy sweet twist on the traditional spice muffin.

Yields 18 Muffins

2 cups all-purpose flour

1 teaspoon baking powder

½ teaspoon baking soda

½ teaspoon salt

½ teaspoon Chinese 5-spice powder

1 cup sugar

¼ cup vegetable or canola oil

¼ cup apricot preserves, melted and cooled

1 teaspoon vanilla

¾ cup whole milk

2 eggs

1 cup diced fresh apricots

1. Preheat oven to 350°F and prepare 18 muffin cups with nonstick spray, or line with paper liners.
2. In a large bowl sift together the flour, baking powder, baking soda, salt, and 5-spice powder. Once sifted, whisk in the sugar until evenly mixed.
3. In a separate bowl add the oil, apricot preserves, vanilla, milk, and eggs. Whisk until the mixture is well combined.
4. Make a well in the center of the dry ingredients and pour in the wet ingredients. With a wooden spoon or spatula, gently fold the mixture until just combined, about 10 strokes. Do not overmix. Gently fold in the apricots, about 3 strokes.
5. Divide the batter evenly between the prepared muffin cups. Bake for 18–20 minutes, or until the muffins spring back when gently pressed in the center and the tops are golden brown. Cool in the pan for 3 minutes, then remove the muffins from the pan to a wire rack to cool to room temperature.

Brown Butter Spice Muffins

If you're looking for a warm, comforting, and chic muffin, then look no further! In this recipe, nutty brown butter and warm spices are baked into a pecan-topped muffin that is sure to please. These muffins have a delicate balance of spices and nutty flavors, and they are perfect for any time of day. Have one with your morning latte or nibble one with your after-dinner coffee—either way it is sure to hit the spot!

Yields 18 Muffins

½ cup butter

2 cups all-purpose flour

1 teaspoon baking powder

½ teaspoon baking soda

½ teaspoon salt

½ teaspoon cinnamon

¼ teaspoon cardamom

¼ teaspoon nutmeg

⅛ teaspoon cloves

1 cup packed light brown sugar

1 teaspoon vanilla

¾ cup whole milk

2 eggs

1 recipe Cinnamon Pecan Streusel (see Chapter 6)

Brown Butter Spread, optional (see Chapter 5)

1. In a small saucepan, warm the butter over medium heat. Cook, stirring constantly, until the butter foams and turns a deep nut-brown color, about 12 minutes. Remove from the heat and cool to room temperature.
2. Preheat oven to 350°F and prepare 18 muffin cups with nonstick spray, or line with paper liners.
3. In a large bowl sift together the flour, baking powder, baking soda, salt, cinnamon, cardamom, nutmeg, and cloves. Once sifted, whisk in the brown sugar until evenly mixed.
4. In a separate bowl add the browned butter, vanilla, milk, and eggs. Whisk until the mixture is well combined.
5. Make a well in the center of the dry ingredients and pour in the wet ingredients. With a wooden spoon or spatula, gently fold the mixture until just combined, about 10–12 strokes. Do not overmix.
6. Divide the batter evenly between the prepared muffin cups, and top with the Cinnamon Pecan Streusel. Bake for 18–20 minutes, or until the muffins spring back when gently pressed in the center and the tops are golden brown. Cool in the pan for 3 minutes, then remove the muffins from the pan to a wire rack to cool to room temperature. Serve with Brown Butter Spread, if desired.

Spiced Chocolate Fudge Swirl Muffins

The rich, spiced chocolate swirl running through the center of these muffins makes them absolutely intoxicating! In this recipe the bright, clean heat of the spicy cayenne pepper combines with the warmth of cinnamon to give the chocolate swirl some extra depth and sophistication. If you don't care for heat, feel free to leave out the cayenne pepper; these muffins will be delicious anyway!

Yields 18 Muffins

2 cups all-purpose flour

1 teaspoon baking powder

½ teaspoon baking soda

½ teaspoon salt

1 cup sugar

½ cup butter, melted and cooled

1 teaspoon vanilla

¾ cup buttermilk

2 eggs

2 tablespoons Dutch-processed cocoa

¼ teaspoon cayenne pepper

¼ teaspoon cinnamon

1. Preheat oven to 350°F and prepare 18 muffin cups with nonstick spray, or line with paper liners.
2. In a large bowl sift together the flour, baking powder, baking soda, and salt. Once sifted, whisk in the sugar until evenly mixed.
3. In a separate bowl add the melted butter, vanilla, buttermilk, and eggs. Whisk until the mixture is well combined.
4. Make a well in the center of the dry ingredients and pour in the wet ingredients. With a wooden spoon or spatula, gently fold the mixture until just combined, about 10 strokes. Do not overmix.
5. Pour ⅓ of the batter into a separate bowl and add the cocoa powder, cayenne pepper, and cinnamon. Fold until evenly mixed, about 5–8 strokes.
6. Spoon half the vanilla batter into the prepared muffin cups. Next add the spiced chocolate batter, then top with the remaining vanilla batter. With a butter knife make a figure-eight pattern in each muffin one time. Bake for 18–20 minutes, or until the muffins spring back when gently pressed in the center and the tops are golden brown. Cool in the pan for 3 minutes, then remove the muffins from the pan to a wire rack to cool to room temperature.

Spicy Coconut Lemongrass Muffins

Coconut and lemongrass are common ingredients in Thai cooking, and the fresh, balanced flavor of that cuisine inspired these muffins. Lemongrass, which has a pleasant, lemony flavor, and cayenne pepper give these coconut muffins an exotic flair! Lemongrass can be found fresh in Asian markets and specialty stores, but it is also sold in dry form. If you can only find it dry, then use 3 tablespoons.

Yields 18 Muffins

¼ cup half-and-half

¾ cup coconut milk

1 stalk lemongrass, cut into 3-inch pieces

2 cups all-purpose flour

1 teaspoon baking powder

½ teaspoon baking soda

½ teaspoon salt

½ teaspoon cayenne pepper

1 cup sugar

⅓ cup vegetable or canola oil

1 teaspoon vanilla

2 eggs

1½ cups sweetened shredded coconut

1 recipe Coconut Glaze (see Chapter 6)

1. In a medium saucepan, add the half-and-half and coconut milk. Lightly crush each piece of lemongrass with a rolling pin and add to the pan. Heat the mixture over medium-low heat until it just comes to a simmer. Cover and let stand until the mixture comes to room temperature. Remove the lemongrass from the liquid, strain, and set aside.

2. Heat oven to 350°F and prepare 18 muffin cups with nonstick spray, or line with paper liners.

3. In a large bowl sift together the flour, baking powder, baking soda, salt, and cayenne pepper. Once sifted, whisk in the sugar until evenly mixed.

4. In a separate bowl add the coconut milk mixture, oil, vanilla, and eggs. Whisk until the mixture is well combined.

5. Make a well in the center of the dry ingredients and pour in the wet ingredients. With a wooden spoon or spatula, gently fold the mixture until just combined, about 10 strokes. Do not overmix. Gently fold in 1 cup of the shredded coconut, about 3 strokes.

6. Divide the batter evenly between the prepared muffin cups. Bake for 18–20 minutes, or until the muffins spring back when gently pressed in the center and the tops are golden brown. Cool in the pan for 3 minutes, then remove the muffins from the pan to a wire rack to cool to room temperature.

7. Once the muffins have cooled, dip the top of each muffin into the Coconut Glaze, and top with the reserved coconut. Let the muffins stand for 1 hour for the glaze to set before serving.

Smoked Gouda Cayenne Corn Muffins

Smoked Gouda Cayenne Corn Muffins

Creamy, smoky, and so tasty, smoked Gouda is an amazing cheese! The flavor is mild but distinctive, and it helps to make these corn muffins creamy and irresistible. The spicy, clean taste of the cayenne pepper heat helps cut any richness, and the cheese helps temper the heat. The combination is absolute perfection!

Yields 18 Muffins

1 cup cornmeal

1 cup all-purpose flour

1 tablespoon white sugar

1½ teaspoons baking powder

¼ teaspoon baking soda

½ teaspoon salt

½ teaspoon cayenne pepper

2 eggs

¼ cup butter, melted and cooled

1 cup buttermilk

1¼ cups shredded smoked Gouda cheese

Smoky Cayenne Butter, optional (see Chapter 5)

1. Preheat oven to 350°F and prepare 18 muffin cups with nonstick spray, or line with paper liners.
2. In a large bowl whisk together the cornmeal, flour, sugar, baking powder, baking soda, salt, and cayenne pepper until well mixed.
3. In a medium bowl add the eggs, butter, and buttermilk, and whisk until evenly combined.
4. Make a well in the center of the dry ingredients and pour in the wet ingredients. With a wooden spoon or spatula, gently fold the mixture until just combined, about 10 strokes. Do not overmix. Add the cheese and fold to evenly distribute, about 3 strokes.
5. Divide the batter evenly between the prepared muffin cups. Bake for 18–20 minutes, or until the muffins spring back when gently pressed in the center and the tops are golden brown. If the tops are too pale, place the muffins under the broiler for 1–2 minutes to give them some color. Cool in the pan for 3 minutes, then remove the muffins from the pan to cool on a wire rack. Enjoy warm with Smoky Cayenne Butter, if desired.

Lemon Serrano Muffins

The tang of fresh lemon and the spicy, yet delectably fruity flavor of serrano chiles make for an unusual but delicious muffin! The serrano flavor is infused throughout this muffin by steeping the chile in the butter, which ensures that the fruity flavor is not reserved for the finely diced pieces, but rather perfumes the entire muffin! You could also make these muffins with jalapeños, if you prefer.

Yields 18 Muffins

⅓ cup butter

1 serrano chile, finely diced

2 cups all-purpose flour

2 teaspoons baking powder

½ teaspoon baking soda

¼ teaspoon salt

¾ cup sugar

¾ cup buttermilk

2 eggs

1 tablespoon freshly grated lemon zest

2 tablespoons fresh lemon juice

1 teaspoon vanilla

1. In a medium skillet over medium heat, combine the butter and the serrano chile. Once the butter has melted and starts to foam, turn off the heat and allow the mixture to come to room temperature.

2. Heat oven to 350°F and prepare 18 muffin cups with nonstick spray, or line with paper liners.

3. In a large bowl sift together the flour, baking powder, baking soda, salt, and sugar.

4. In a medium bowl combine the butter mixture, buttermilk, eggs, lemon zest, lemon juice, and vanilla. Whisk until smooth.

5. Make a well in the center of the dry ingredients and pour in the wet ingredients. With a wooden spoon or spatula, gently fold the mixture until just combined, about 10–12 strokes. Do not overmix.

6. Divide the batter evenly between the prepared muffin cups. Bake for 18–20 minutes, or until the muffins spring back when gently pressed in the center. Cool in the pan for 3 minutes, then remove the muffins from the pan to a wire rack to cool completely.

Chipotle Peanut Butter Chip Muffins

In this recipe you get a double dose of peanut butter with a peanut butter–flavored muffin studded with peanut butter chips. To help cut the richness of the peanut butter and to add a little zing, a small amount of dry chipotle powder is added. The heat of the chipotle is pleasantly tingly with a smoky finish and is not overwhelming—ensuring that these muffins make a wonderfully upscale and unusual snack or dessert!

Yields 18 Muffins

2 cups all-purpose flour

½ cup sugar

¼ cup packed light brown sugar

1 teaspoon baking powder

½ teaspoon baking soda

½ teaspoon salt

½ teaspoon chipotle powder

¼ cup butter, melted and cooled

½ cup peanut butter, melted and cooled

1 teaspoon vanilla

1 cup buttermilk

2 eggs

1 cup peanut butter chips

1 recipe Peanut Butter Drizzle (see Chapter 6)

1. Preheat oven to 350°F and prepare 18 muffin cups with nonstick spray, or line with paper liners.
2. In a large bowl sift together the flour, sugar, brown sugar, baking powder, baking soda, salt, and chipotle powder.
3. In a separate bowl add the butter, peanut butter, vanilla, buttermilk, and eggs. Whisk until the mixture is well combined.
4. Make a well in the center of the dry ingredients and pour in the wet ingredients. With a wooden spoon or spatula, gently fold the mixture until just combined, about 10 strokes. Do not overmix. Add the peanut butter chips and fold to mix, about 3 strokes.
5. Divide the batter evenly between the prepared muffin cups. Bake for 18–20 minutes, or until the muffins spring back when gently pressed in the center and the tops are golden brown. Cool in the pan for 3 minutes, then remove the muffins from the pan to a wire rack to cool to room temperature.
6. Once the muffins are cooled completely, drizzle them with the Peanut Butter Drizzle. Allow the drizzle to set, about 1 hour, before serving.

Pear, Date, and Blue Cheese Muffins

Looking for a muffin that is a delicate balance of sweet and savory? These muffins, loaded with bits of fresh pear, chewy dates, and tangy blue cheese, are perfect to serve at both a dinner party or a simple dinner with your family. If baked in a mini-muffin pan, they also make an elegant appetizer or can be served as a lovely addition to a fruit and cheese plate.

Yields 18 Muffins

¼ cup cornmeal

1¾ cups all-purpose flour

¼ cup white sugar

1½ teaspoons baking powder

¼ teaspoon baking soda

½ teaspoon salt

2 eggs

⅓ cup butter, melted and cooled

1 cup buttermilk

½ cup crumbled blue cheese

½ cup chopped dried dates

1 pear, peeled, cored and diced

1. Preheat oven to 350°F and prepare 18 muffin cups with nonstick spray, or line with paper liners.
2. In a large bowl whisk together the cornmeal, flour, sugar, baking powder, baking soda, and salt until well mixed.
3. In a medium bowl add the eggs, butter, and buttermilk, and whisk until evenly combined.
4. Make a well in the center of the dry ingredients and pour in the wet ingredients. With a wooden spoon or spatula, gently fold the mixture until just combined, about 10 strokes. Do not overmix. Add the blue cheese, dates, and pear, and fold to evenly distribute, about 3 strokes.
5. Divide the batter evenly between the prepared muffin cups. Bake for 18–20 minutes, or until the muffins spring back when gently pressed in the center and the tops are golden brown. If the tops are too pale, place the muffins under the broiler for 1–2 minutes to give them some color. Cool in the pan for 3 minutes, then remove the muffins from the pan to cool on a wire rack. Enjoy warm.

Pear, Date, and Blue Cheese Muffins

Fresh Zucchini Muffins

Freshly grated zucchini is typically found in zucchini bread, but here it makes for muffins that are moist, exceptionally hearty, and that pack some unexpected vegetable goodness! Perfect for grab-and-go meals that are not only tasty but gourmet, these muffins can be made even better if you add ½ cup of chopped walnuts or pecans for some added texture and nutty flavor.

Yields 18 Muffins

2 cups all-purpose flour

1 teaspoon salt

½ teaspoon baking soda

½ teaspoon baking powder

½ teaspoon cinnamon

1 cup sugar

½ cup vegetable oil

2 eggs

⅔ cup whole milk

1 cup fresh zucchini, grated

1 recipe Streusel Crumble (see Chapter 6)

1. Preheat oven to 350°F and prepare 18 muffin cups with nonstick spray, or line with paper liners.
2. In a large bowl sift together the flour, salt, baking soda, baking powder, and cinnamon. Add the sugar and whisk until well combined.
3. In a separate bowl combine the vegetable oil, eggs, and milk. Whisk until the mixture is well combined.
4. Make a well in the center of the dry ingredients and pour in the wet ingredients. With a wooden spoon or spatula, gently fold the mixture until just combined, about 10 strokes. Do not overmix. Add the zucchini and fold to mix, about 3 strokes.
5. Divide the batter evenly between the prepared muffin cups, and top with the Streusel Crumble. Bake for 18–20 minutes, or until the muffins spring back when gently pressed in the center and the tops are golden brown. Cool in the pan for 3 minutes, then remove the muffins from the pan to a wire rack to cool to room temperature.

Rosemary Carrot Muffins

Carrots and rosemary play well off one another and their subtle flavors and pungent aromas are often found in savory soups and salads. Now those flavors combine in a moist corn muffin that has a unique savory flavor and a lightly sweet finish. A little Greek-style yogurt is used to add a little tang to these muffins and to help keep the flavors balanced.

Yields 18 Muffins

1½ cups all-purpose flour

½ cup cornmeal

¾ teaspoon baking powder

¾ teaspoon baking soda

½ teaspoon salt

¼ teaspoon smoked paprika

⅛ teaspoon ground ginger

2 tablespoons packed light brown sugar

⅓ cup canola or vegetable oil

½ cup buttermilk

¼ cup whole-milk Greek-style yogurt

1 tablespoon freshly minced rosemary

2 eggs

½ cup finely grated carrot

1. Preheat oven to 350°F and prepare 18 muffin cups with nonstick spray, or line with paper liners.
2. In a large bowl sift together the flour, cornmeal, baking powder, baking soda, salt, smoked paprika, and ginger. Once sifted, whisk in the brown sugar until evenly mixed.
3. In a separate bowl add the oil, buttermilk, yogurt, rosemary, and eggs. Whisk until the mixture is well combined.
4. Make a well in the center of the dry ingredients and pour in the wet ingredients. With a wooden spoon or spatula, gently fold the mixture until just combined, about 10 strokes. Do not overmix. Add the carrots and fold to evenly distribute, about 3 strokes.
5. Divide the batter evenly between the prepared muffin cups. Bake for 18–20 minutes, or until the muffins spring back when gently pressed in the center and the tops are golden brown. If the tops are too pale, place the muffins under the broiler for 1–2 minutes to give them some color. Cool in the pan for 3 minutes, then remove the muffins from the pan to cool on a wire rack. Enjoy warm.

Pepper Jack Chorizo Muffins

Pepper Jack Chorizo Muffins

Spanish chorizo, the cured version of the Mexican sausage, has a bold, spicy flavor and a bright red color. In this muffin, crisp bits of chorizo are blended into a batter made moist and flavorful with a dose of pepper jack cheese. These muffins are a wonderful accompaniment to hearty stews, seafood, and grilled meats. If you make them in a mini-muffin pan they're also a wonderful addition to a tapas party!

Yields 18 Muffins

1 cup diced Spanish chorizo

½ cup cornmeal

1½ cups all-purpose flour

1 tablespoon sugar

1½ teaspoons baking powder

¼ teaspoon baking soda

½ teaspoon salt

½ teaspoon smoked paprika

2 eggs

⅓ cup butter, melted and cooled

1 cup buttermilk

1¼ cups shredded pepper jack cheese

1. In a medium skillet over medium heat, add the chorizo. Cook, stirring often, until the sausage begins to crisp around the edges and has rendered some of its fat. Remove the sausage from the pan and drain on paper towels until ready to use.
2. Preheat oven to 350°F and prepare 18 muffin cups with nonstick spray, or line with paper liners.
3. In a large bowl whisk together the cornmeal, flour, sugar, baking powder, baking soda, salt, and smoked paprika until well mixed.
4. In a medium bowl add the eggs, butter, and buttermilk, and whisk until evenly combined.
5. Make a well in the center of the dry ingredients and pour in the wet ingredients. With a wooden spoon or spatula, gently fold the mixture until just combined, about 10 strokes. Do not overmix. Add the chorizo and pepper jack cheese and fold to evenly distribute, about 3 strokes.
6. Divide the batter evenly between the prepared muffin cups. Bake for 18–20 minutes, or until the muffins spring back when gently pressed in the center and the tops are golden brown. If the tops are too pale, place the muffins under the broiler for 1–2 minutes to give them some color. Cool in the pan for 3 minutes, then remove the muffins from the pan to cool on a wire rack. Enjoy warm.

Salted Caramel–Glazed Cherry Muffins

Fresh, slightly sour cherries and salted caramel are an underrated combination, but they are truly mouthwatering! The tartness of the fresh cherry combined with the salty sweetness of the caramel creates a harmonious balance of flavor, and in this recipe it is utterly addicting! If you'd like, feel free to add ½ cup of toasted almonds to this recipe for some extra crunch.

Yields 18 Muffins

2 cups all-purpose flour

1 teaspoon baking powder

½ teaspoon baking soda

½ teaspoon salt

¼ teaspoon cinnamon

1 cup sugar

⅓ cup butter, melted and cooled

1 teaspoon vanilla

¼ teaspoon almond extract

¾ cup buttermilk

¼ cup cherry preserves, melted and cooled

2 eggs

1 cup fresh pitted cherries, cut in half

1 recipe Salted Caramel Glaze (see Chapter 6)

¼ cup finely chopped dry cherries

Salted Caramel Butter, optional (see Chapter 5)

1. Preheat oven to 350°F and prepare 18 muffin cups with nonstick spray, or line with paper liners.
2. In a large bowl sift together the flour, baking powder, baking soda, salt, and cinnamon. Once sifted, whisk in the sugar until evenly mixed.
3. In a separate bowl add the melted butter, vanilla, almond extract, buttermilk, cherry preserves, and eggs. Whisk until the mixture is well combined.
4. Make a well in the center of the dry ingredients and pour in the wet ingredients. With a wooden spoon or spatula, gently fold the mixture until just combined, about 10 strokes. Do not overmix. Add the cherries into the batter and fold to evenly distribute, about 3 strokes.
5. Divide the batter evenly between the prepared muffin cups. Bake for 18–20 minutes, or until the muffins spring back when gently pressed in the center and the tops are golden brown. Cool in the pan for 3 minutes, then remove the muffins from the pan to a wire rack to cool to room temperature.
6. Once cooled, dip the tops of the muffins into the Salted Caramel Glaze, allowing the excess to drip off. While the glaze is still wet, sprinkle a few pieces of chopped dried cherries over the top. Place the muffins on a cooling rack and allow the glaze to set, about 1 hour, before serving. Serve with Salted Caramel Butter, if desired.

Spiced Nut Muffins

This muffin recipe contains a delicious combination of chopped and toasted hazelnuts, almonds, and pecans with a hint of spicy cayenne pepper that will have nut lovers swooning! Inspired by sweet and spicy nut mixes that are popular for snacking, this recipe uses a little whole-wheat pastry flour to add another layer of nutty flavor. Whole-wheat pastry flour has a lighter texture than traditional whole-wheat flour but has all the earthy flavor that this gourmet dish craves!

Yields 18 Muffins

⅓ cup finely chopped pecans

⅓ cup finely chopped hazelnuts

⅓ cup finely chopped almonds

1½ cups all-purpose flour

½ cup whole-wheat pastry flour

¾ teaspoon baking powder

¾ teaspoon baking soda

½ teaspoon salt

½ teaspoon cinnamon

¼ teaspoon cayenne pepper

¼ teaspoon cardamom

1 cup packed light brown sugar

⅓ cup canola or vegetable oil

1 teaspoon vanilla

1 cup buttermilk

2 eggs

1 recipe Almond Brown Sugar Topping (see Chapter 6)

1. Preheat oven to 350°F and prepare 18 muffin cups with nonstick spray, or line with paper liners.
2. On a small baking sheet lined with parchment paper, spread the chopped nuts in an even layer. Bake for 6–8 minutes, stirring every couple of minutes to ensure even toasting. Once the nuts are slightly darker in color and fragrant, pull them from the oven and allow them to cool.
3. In a large bowl sift together the flour, whole-wheat pastry flour, baking powder, baking soda, salt, cinnamon, cayenne pepper, and cardamom. Once sifted, whisk in the brown sugar until evenly mixed.
4. In a separate bowl add the oil, vanilla, buttermilk, and eggs. Whisk until the mixture is well combined.
5. Make a well in the center of the dry ingredients and pour in the wet ingredients. With a wooden spoon or spatula, gently fold the mixture until just combined, about 10 strokes. Do not overmix. Add the toasted nuts into the batter and fold to evenly distribute, about 3 strokes.
6. Divide the batter evenly between the prepared muffin cups, and top with the Almond Brown Sugar Topping. Bake for 18–20 minutes, or until the muffins spring back when gently pressed in the center and the tops are golden brown. Cool in the pan for 3 minutes, then remove the muffins from the pan to cool on a wire rack. Enjoy warm.

Pumpkin Gruyère Muffins

Most people think of pumpkin and immediately think of sweet recipes for things like pie, cake, and bread. But pumpkin is also a delicious ingredient when used in savory cooking. This moist, savory muffin combines the mild, slightly sweet flavor of pumpkin with the nutty, salty flavor of Gruyère cheese. The flavors here are reminiscent of a cheese fondue, but are a little more robust and hearty. And, to make it even better, these muffins go great with cocktails!

Yields 18 Muffins

½ cup cornmeal

1½ cups all-purpose flour

1½ teaspoons baking powder

¼ teaspoon baking soda

½ teaspoon salt

½ teaspoon mustard powder

1 tablespoon sugar

2 eggs

⅓ cup butter, melted and cooled

½ cup whole milk

½ cup pumpkin purée

1¼ cups shredded Gruyère cheese

1 recipe Parmesan Crumble (see Chapter 6)

1. Preheat oven to 350°F and prepare 18 muffin cups with nonstick spray, or line with paper liners.
2. In a large bowl whisk together the cornmeal, flour, baking powder, baking soda, salt, mustard powder, and sugar until well mixed.
3. In a medium bowl add the eggs, butter, milk, and pumpkin purée, and whisk until evenly combined.
4. Make a well in the center of the dry ingredients and pour in the wet ingredients. With a wooden spoon or spatula, gently fold the mixture until just combined, about 10 strokes. Do not overmix. Add the shredded cheese and fold to evenly distribute, about 3 strokes.
5. Divide the batter evenly between the prepared muffin cups, and top with the Parmesan Crumble. Bake for 18–20 minutes, or until the muffins spring back when gently pressed in the center and the tops are golden brown. If the tops are too pale, place the muffins under the broiler for 1–2 minutes to give them some color. Cool in the pan for 3 minutes, then remove the muffins from the pan to cool on a wire rack. Enjoy warm.

Apricot Jalapeño Muffins

A little sweet, a little spicy, and so very good, these high-brow Apricot Jalapeño Muffins are sure to add a little zip to your day! These tender corn muffins go well with comfort foods like fried chicken, roasted turkey, or baked ham. But you can also enjoy these all on their own with some good salted butter or some Toasted Pecan Apricot Spread (Chapter 5).

Yields 18 Muffins

1 tablespoon butter

1 jalapeño, finely minced

½ cup cornmeal

1½ cups all-purpose flour

1 teaspoon baking powder

½ teaspoon baking soda

½ teaspoon salt

2 tablespoons sugar

⅓ cup vegetable or canola oil

¼ cup apricot preserves, melted and cooled

¾ cup half-and-half

2 eggs

½ cup finely diced dried apricots

Toasted Pecan Apricot Spread, optional (see Chapter 5)

1. In a medium skillet, warm the butter over medium heat until it foams. Add the jalapeño and cook, stirring frequently, until softened, about 2 minutes. Remove the pan from the heat and allow to cool to room temperature.
2. Preheat oven to 350°F and prepare 18 muffin cups with nonstick spray, or line with paper liners.
3. In a large bowl sift together the cornmeal, flour, baking powder, baking soda, and salt. Once sifted, whisk in the sugar until evenly mixed.
4. In a separate bowl add the oil, apricot preserves, half-and-half, and eggs. Whisk until the mixture is well combined.
5. Make a well in the center of the dry ingredients and pour in the wet ingredients. With a wooden spoon or spatula, gently fold the mixture until just combined, about 10 strokes. Do not overmix. Gently fold in the jalapeños and diced dried apricots, about 3 strokes.
6. Divide the batter evenly between the prepared muffin cups. Bake for 18–20 minutes, or until the muffins spring back when gently pressed in the center and the tops are golden brown. Cool in the pan for 3 minutes, then remove the muffins from the pan to a wire rack to cool to room temperature. Serve with butter or Toasted Pecan Apricot Spread, if desired.

PART 3

To Top It Off

A muffin alone is nice, but add a few flourishes and a *moufflet* becomes absolutely lovely!

Nothing takes a sweet or savory muffin from unremarkable to exceptional faster than a well-placed spread, crumble, or glaze. From chocolate to chipotle, from smoked paprika to salted caramel, no matter the occasion there is something here to suit all! A luscious herb-laced butter can make a batch of plain corn muffins the most popular part of a meal. A plain fruit muffin becomes a rustic crowd pleaser with a buttery crumble tumbled over the top. Think of it as gilding the lily! These additions take mere moments to make, create a stunning visual impact, and provide another avenue to showcase some gourmet flavors and techniques.

So remember, it is easy to dress up your muffins with some finesse flavors when you top it off right!

CHAPTER 5

Sensational Spreads

Nothing complements a high-end muffin better than a high-end spread!

When it comes to your beautifully crafted, artisanal muffins, why use plain old butter when you can take it to the next step? Making a gourmet spread or butter is a small detail that can deliver big results! Nutty brown butter, dried figs, tangy blue cheese, and fragrant lavender are just a few of the many ingredients that can be incorporated into delicious spreads that will become a showcase for your muffins! Even homemade bacon jam, scented with spices and bourbon, can be whipped into a creamy spread perfect for any occasion! A good spread, like a good muffin, should be made from the best-quality ingredients possible, and those ingredients should be used to their best advantage. So whether your *moufflet* is sweet, savory, or something in between, the spreads found in this chapter will take even a plain muffin and turn it into something mouthwateringly divine. So get ready to dress up your baking with some sensational spreads!

Compound Herb Butter

Fresh herbs and creamy butter make this spread an elegant addition to any meal—and more than exceptional when spread on a warm muffin. You can use any herbs that you like in this recipe, but the combination used here complement a wide variety of muffins including Zucchini Cheese Muffins (Chapter 3), Rosemary Olive Oil Muffins (Chapter 3), or Crab Salad Corn Muffins (Chapter 3). A little lemon zest helps keep the flavor of this butter fresh and light!

Yields approximately 1 cup

1 cup butter, at room temperature
3 tablespoons fresh chives, finely chopped
2 tablespoons fresh thyme, finely chopped
2 tablespoons fresh parsley, finely chopped
1 tablespoon fresh sage, finely chopped
½ teaspoon grated lemon zest
½ teaspoon fresh cracked black pepper
¼ teaspoon salt

1. In a medium bowl, lightly beat the butter with a spatula until softened. Add the chives, thyme, parsley, sage, lemon zest, pepper, and salt, and mix until evenly distributed.
2. Scoop the butter onto the center of a sheet of parchment paper that is approximately 12 × 17 inches. Roll into a log by folding the parchment over the butter and pressing the butter into a log shape. Roll the parchment around the butter and chill until the butter is firm, about 2 hours.

Whipped Honey Lavender Butter

Lavender has a sharp floral flavor and a distinct aroma, and today it is found in a wide array of upscale baked goods. Here, butter is whipped with a little honey and some dried lavender to create a light and creamy spread perfect for all kinds of muffins. This recipe is delicious on sweet muffins like Cornmeal Buttermilk Muffins (Chapter 1), but it makes a particularly good spread for sweet cornbread, too!

Yields approximately 1 cup

1 cup butter, at room temperature
2 tablespoons honey
1½ teaspoons dried lavender, crushed
Pinch of salt

1. In a medium bowl combine the butter, honey, dried lavender, and salt. Whip the butter until it is lighter in color, about 5 minutes by hand or 2 minutes with a mixer on high speed.
2. Transfer the butter into a serving dish and chill for at least 2 hours so the flavors can develop. Allow the butter to set at room temperature for 30 minutes before serving.

Whipped Honey Lavender Butter

Salted Caramel Butter

Salted caramel has a warm, earthy flavor that is sparked by a touch of flaky sea salt. Here that tasty caramel is beaten into butter with a hint of vanilla to create an upscale spread perfect for a gourmet muffin. This butter is especially good on spiced muffins, or muffins with a fruity flavor, such as apple, pear, or cherry, like the Salted Caramel–Glazed Cherry Muffins (Chapter 4), or the Cinnamon Apple Corn Muffins (Chapter 1).

Yields approximately 2 cups

½ cup sugar

1 tablespoon water

1 tablespoon light corn syrup

⅓ cup heavy cream

2 tablespoons unsalted butter

¾ teaspoon sea salt, crushed

1 cup butter

½ teaspoon vanilla

1. In a medium saucepan with deep sides over medium-high heat, combine the sugar, water, and corn syrup. Brush down the sides of the pan with a wet pastry brush until it begins to bubble.
2. Bring the mixture to a full boil and cook until the mixture becomes dark amber in color and smells like caramel, about 6 minutes. Remove the saucepan from the heat and carefully whisk in the cream, butter, and sea salt.
3. Allow the caramel to cool completely to room temperature, then chill for 1 hour.
4. In a large bowl combine the salted caramel, butter, and vanilla. Beat until the mixture is smooth. Transfer the mixture to a bowl and chill for at least 2 hours before serving.

Brown Butter Spread

Brown butter has a toasty, rich flavor. In this recipe, rich brown butter is mixed with cream cheese and just a little powdered sugar to create a unique blend that's sure to impress anyone you serve it to! If you like, you can also add a little orange zest or cinnamon to add some extra flavor. This spread is especially good on the Brown Butter and Oat Muffins in Chapter 2.

Yields approximately 1 cup

¾ cup butter, at room temperature

¼ cup cream cheese, at room temperature

3 tablespoons powdered sugar

1 teaspoon vanilla

1. In a small saucepan over medium heat, add ½ cup of the butter. Cook, stirring constantly, until the butter foams and turns a deep nut-brown color, about 12 minutes. Remove from the heat and cool to room temperature.
2. In a medium bowl combine the browned butter, the remaining ¼ cup of butter, the cream cheese, powdered sugar, and vanilla. Mix until all the ingredients are well combined.
3. Transfer the spread into a serving dish and chill for at least 1 hour before serving.

Cinnamon Walnut Cream Cheese Spread

Buttery walnuts and warm cinnamon make this spread a knockout, particularly around the holidays on muffins like Gingerbread Crumble Muffins (Chapter 1) or Pumpkin Caramel Muffins (Chapter 1)! Toasting the walnuts before adding them to this spread unlocks all their flavor and also adds a toasty finish to this recipe. If you prefer, you could also use toasted pecans, almonds, or a combination of different toasted nuts!

Yields approximately 1 cup

¾ cup cream cheese, at room temperature

¼ cup butter, at room temperature

3 tablespoons honey

½ cup toasted walnuts, finely chopped

½ teaspoon cinnamon

½ teaspoon vanilla

In a medium bowl combine the cream cheese, butter, and honey. Beat until the mixture is smooth, then add the walnuts, cinnamon, and vanilla, and mix until well combined. Transfer to a serving bowl and chill for at least 1 hour before serving.

Pimento Cheese Spread with Sharp Cheddar Ale Muffins (see Chapter 3)

Pimento Cheese Spread

Pimento cheese is a Southern food staple and this creamy blend of cheese and pimentos makes a wonderful spread for all manner of breads and muffins such as Sharp Cheddar Ale Muffins and the Spiced Pimento Cheese Muffins from Chapter 3. This recipe calls for a touch of cream cheese, which makes this pimento cheese easy to spread. This tastes best if given a chance to chill overnight, but let it warm up slightly before serving because the cheese will have a more robust flavor, and it will spread more easily, if it is not cold.

Yields approximately 1½ cups

¼ cup mayonnaise

2 tablespoons cream cheese, at room temperature

2 teaspoons hot sauce

¼ teaspoon Worcestershire sauce

2 cups shredded sharp Cheddar cheese

¼ cup diced pimentos, drained well

1. In the work bowl of a food processor combine the mayonnaise, cream cheese, hot sauce, and Worcestershire sauce, and pulse until creamy, about 5 pulses. Add 1 cup of the shredded cheese and pulse to mix, about 5 pulses.
2. Transfer the mixture into a medium bowl along with the remaining shredded cheese and the pimentos. Mix until well combined, then chill for at least 2 hours or overnight. Allow the mixture to stand at room temperature for 30 minutes before serving.

Toasted Pecan Apricot Spread

Toasting pecans releases their essential oils and gives them an earthy flavor. When you combine that earthy taste with the robust sweetness of dried apricots, you create a spread that's an absolute winner! The crisp nuts and chewy fruit found in this recipe ensures that every bite will have unbelievable flavor and texture. This spread is lovely on sweet muffins like Peach Pecan Streusel (Chapter 2) or Apricot Jalapeño Muffins (Chapter 4), but is also very nice on cornbread.

Yields approximately 1 cup

½ cup cream cheese, at room temperature

½ cup butter, at room temperature

3 tablespoons packed light brown sugar

½ cup toasted pecans, finely chopped

¼ cup dried apricots, finely chopped

¼ teaspoon cinnamon

½ teaspoon vanilla

In a medium bowl combine the cream cheese, butter, and brown sugar. Beat until the mixture is smooth, then add the pecans, apricots, cinnamon, and vanilla, and mix until well combined. Transfer to a serving bowl and chill for at least 1 hour before serving.

Candied Jalapeño Spread

Candied jalapeños are simply jalapeño slices that have been preserved in a spicy sugar syrup that gives them a tangy sweet flavor and a burst of heat! They are available in specialty stores or online, and they are utterly irresistible! This spread is best if made the day before you plan to serve it so the flavors will have a chance to meld. If you prefer a sweeter spread, simply leave out the crumbled bacon. Try this spread on your favorite cornbread recipe, or for something a little daring spread some on the Chipotle Peanut Butter Chip Muffins in Chapter 4!

Yields approximately 1½ cups

1 cup cream cheese, at room temperature
½ cup candied jalapeños, finely chopped
2 tablespoons candied jalapeño pickling liquid
4 strips bacon, cooked crisp and finely crumbled

In a medium bowl combine the cream cheese, candied jalapeños, pickling liquid, and bacon, and mix until well combined. Transfer to a serving bowl and chill overnight before serving.

Chipotle Cream Cheese

Smoky chipotle peppers add rich flavor and a touch of heat whenever they are added. In this recipe, the combination of chipotle and cumin imbues this creamy spread with an earthy flavor that's out of this world. This spread pairs well with hearty muffins such as the Spicy Sausage and Cheddar Muffins (Chapter 3) or the Bell Pepper and Cheddar Corn Muffins (Chapter 3). If you want to pump up the heat, feel free to add a few drops of your favorite hot sauce!

Yields approximately 1 cup

1 cup cream cheese, at room temperature
1 chipotle peppers in adobo, finely minced
1 teaspoon adobo sauce
½ teaspoon cumin
1 tablespoon honey
½ teaspoon paprika

In a medium bowl combine the cream cheese, chipotle peppers, adobo sauce, cumin, and honey until evenly mixed. Transfer to a serving bowl and dust the top with the paprika. Chill for at least 2 hours, or overnight, before serving.

Garlic-Infused Butter

When raw, garlic has a very strong flavor, but once it's roasted it becomes mellow, sweet, and soft. Here roasted garlic is combined with butter and herbs to make a delicious compound spread that will have your guests thinking you spent all day slaving away! This spread is out of this world when spread on Garlic Chive Buttermilk Muffins (Chapter 3), and is also lovely on Feta and Herb Muffins (Chapter 3). Besides serving this butter with your favorite muffins, try a small slice of this butter over freshly grilled meats.

Yields approximately 1 cup

1 bulb garlic

1 tablespoon olive oil

1 cup butter, at room temperature

1 tablespoon fresh chopped parsley

1 tablespoon fresh chopped chives

½ teaspoon fresh chopped thyme

¼ teaspoon fresh cracked black pepper

⅛ teaspoon salt

1. Preheat oven to 375°F.
2. Peel off all the paper surrounding the bulb of garlic, leaving just the papers on the individual cloves intact. Carefully slice off the top of the garlic bulb so that the garlic cloves are exposed, about ¼ inch.
3. Place the garlic, cut side up, on a baking sheet and drizzle with olive oil. Cover with foil and bake for 45–60 minutes, or until the garlic is golden brown and very soft. Cool to room temperature, then squeeze the garlic into a bowl. Mash the garlic with a fork until it forms a smooth paste.
4. In a medium bowl add 2 tablespoons of the garlic mixture, the butter, parsley, chives, thyme, pepper, and salt. Mix until well combined. Scoop the butter onto the center of a sheet of parchment paper that is approximately 12 × 17 inches. Roll into a log by folding the parchment over the butter and pressing the butter into a log shape. Roll the parchment around the butter and chill until the butter is firm, about 2 hours.

Smoky Cayenne Butter

Making compound butter with lots of bold spices is an easy way to add a touch of elegance and a lot of flavor! This spread would also make an excellent gift, tucked into a basket of savory muffins such as the Smoked Gouda Cayenne Corn Muffins in Chapter 4 or the Cheesy Shrimp Muffins in Chapter 3. Depending on your taste you may want to add more or less cayenne pepper to this recipe. Feel free to adjust the spices until you find just the right balance for you!

Yields approximately 1 cup

1 cup butter, at room temperature
½ teaspoon smoked paprika
½ teaspoon cayenne pepper
¼ teaspoon coriander
¼ teaspoon freshly cracked black pepper

1. In a medium bowl combine the butter, smoked paprika, cayenne pepper, coriander, and black pepper until evenly mixed.
2. Scoop the butter onto the center of a sheet of parchment paper that is approximately 12 × 17 inches. Roll into a log by folding the parchment over the butter and pressing the butter into a log shape. Roll the parchment around the butter and chill until the butter is firm, about 2 hours.

Fig Ricotta Spread

Dried figs are sweet, sticky, and have a pleasant chewiness to them. In this spread, dried figs and fig preserves are mixed into a rich ricotta and cream cheese base. The final touch is a kiss of honey and a dash of vanilla. This spread would make an elegant addition to a brunch buffet or as an accompaniment to a blue cheese–flavored muffin, such as the Pear, Date, and Blue Cheese Muffins in Chapter 4.

Yields approximately 1 cup

½ cup ricotta cheese, at room temperature
¼ cup cream cheese, at room temperature
2 tablespoons honey
1 tablespoon powdered sugar
¼ cup fig preserves
¼ cup dried figs, finely chopped
½ teaspoon vanilla

In a medium bowl combine the ricotta, cream cheese, honey, and powdered sugar. Beat until the mixture is smooth, then stir in the fig preserves, dried figs, and vanilla, and mix until well combined. Transfer to a serving bowl and chill for at least 1 hour before serving.

Fig Ricotta Spread with Cornmeal Buttermilk Muffins (see Chapter 1)

Garlic Chile Cream Cheese Spread

Toasted garlic and roasted green chiles give this spread an abundance of zesty Southwestern flair! Blending this spread in the food processor is key to its smooth and creamy texture. Once blended, just add a little whole garlic and green chile back in for texture, and this spread will be beautiful! This is fabulous with hearty muffins flavored with tangy cheese and cornbread such as Queso Blanco Corn Muffins (Chapter 3).

Yields approximately 1 cup

2 tablespoons butter

2 cloves garlic, finely minced

¾ cup cream cheese, at room temperature

¼ cup roasted green chiles, diced

½ teaspoon smoked paprika

¼ teaspoon salt

1. In a small saucepan over medium-low heat, warm the butter. Once the butter foams add the garlic and cook, stirring constantly, until the garlic is golden brown, about 2 minutes. Remove the pan from the heat and let the garlic cool to room temperature.
2. In the work bowl of a food processor add ⅔ of the browned garlic, the cream cheese, 3 tablespoons of the green chiles, ¼ teaspoon of the smoked paprika, and the salt. Pulse until all the ingredients are well combined, about 8 pulses.
3. Transfer the spread into a bowl and stir in the remaining garlic and chile. Smooth the top of the spread and dust the remaining smoked paprika over the top. Chill for at least 1 hour before serving.

Jalapeño Cheddar Spread

Jalapeños have a naturally fruity flavor, and that flavor is enhanced by roasting. Here fresh jalapeño is roasted until it is very tender, then it is mixed into an irresistibly cheesy spread. While sharp Cheddar is used in this recipe for its tangy flavor, you could substitute different cheeses, such as quesadilla or queso fresco, if you prefer. This spread makes a perfect match for the King Ranch Chicken Muffins in Chapter 3.

Yields approximately 1½ cups

2 medium jalapeños

¾ cup cream cheese, at room temperature

½ cup shredded sharp Cheddar cheese

¼ teaspoon cumin

¼ teaspoon smoked paprika

¼ teaspoon fresh cracked black pepper

⅛ teaspoon salt

1. Place a very heavy skillet—cast iron is excellent for this—over medium heat. Once the pan is very hot, about 4 minutes, add the jalapeños. Roast, turning often, until the flesh is tender and the skins are charred and blistered, about 8 minutes.

2. Transfer the hot peppers to a bowl and cover with plastic wrap to trap the steam. Allow to cool to room temperature. Once cooled, peel away the charred skins, but do not rinse; then remove the seeds and finely chop the flesh.

3. In a medium-sized microwave-safe bowl, heat the cream cheese until it is warm but not melted. Add the Cheddar cheese and stir to combine. Add the jalapeño, cumin, paprika, pepper, and salt, and mix well.

4. Transfer the mixture to a serving bowl and chill for at least 1 hour before serving.

Blue Cheese Walnut Spread with Ham and Swiss Muffins (see Chapter 3)

Blue Cheese Walnut Spread

Pungent blue cheese is, for those who love it, an amazing ingredient. With a slightly tangy, rich flavor, a little really goes a long way. In this recipe, beautiful blue cheese is combined with toasted walnuts and a touch of honey for a spread that would be a lovely addition to a savory muffin like the Ham and Currant Muffins (Chapter 3), Ham and Swiss Muffins (Chapter 3), or Caramelized Onion and Bacon Muffins (Chapter 3). If you prefer, you can reduce or increase the amount of blue cheese to suit your taste.

Yields approximately 1½ cups

1 cup cream cheese, at room temperature
½ cup crumbled blue cheese
2 tablespoons honey
½ cup chopped, toasted walnuts

In a medium bowl combine the cream cheese, blue cheese, and honey until well combined. Add the walnuts and mix well. Transfer to a serving bowl and chill overnight before serving.

Rhubarb Preserves Cream Cheese Spread

Fresh rhubarb, which can be found in most produce markets in the spring, has a very tart flavor and is typically cooked down with sugar and other sweeter fruits like strawberries to cut the tartness. However, this recipe uses a timesaving, flavor-boosting shortcut in the form of rhubarb jam, which can be found in gourmet stores and online. Pair this spread with fruity muffins like the Strawberries and Cream Muffins in Chapter 2 or the Vanilla Bean Apple Muffins in Chapter 1.

Yields approximately 1½ cups

1 cup cream cheese, at room temperature
3 tablespoons butter
½ cup rhubarb preserves
2 tablespoons honey
¼ teaspoon cinnamon
¼ teaspoon vanilla

In a medium bowl combine the cream cheese, butter, rhubarb preserves, honey, cinnamon, and vanilla, and mix until well combined. Transfer to a serving bowl and chill overnight before serving.

Chorizo Cheddar Cream Cheese

Mexican chorizo is a spicy sausage that can be found fresh in most meat markets. Its bold red color and rich flavor make it a particularly popular ingredient in Tex-Mex cooking. Here that bold flavor is whipped into a creamy, dreamy spread perfect for savory muffins like the Chipotle Swirl Corn Muffins and the Pepper Jack Chorizo Muffins in Chapter 4. If you like, you can serve this spread warm; just bake it in an oven-safe dish until it is bubbling hot, about 15–20 minutes!

Yields approximately 1½ cups

½ cup chorizo

¾ cup cream cheese, at room temperature

¼ cup mayonnaise

½ cup shredded sharp Cheddar cheese

¼ teaspoon cumin

¼ teaspoon coriander

¼ teaspoon freshly cracked black pepper

⅛ teaspoon salt

1. Place a very heavy skillet—cast iron is excellent for this—over medium heat. Once the pan is hot, add the chorizo. Cook, stirring often, until the meat is fully cooked, about 8–10 minutes.
2. Transfer the hot chorizo to a bowl and add the cream cheese, mayonnaise, Cheddar cheese, cumin, coriander, pepper, and salt, and mix well.
3. Transfer the mixture to a serving bowl and chill for at least 1 hour before serving.

Smoky Bacon Spread

Bacon has been the "it" ingredient for the last few years and for good reason. Smoky, fatty, and bursting with flavor, bacon truly makes anything better. This spread uses a homemade bourbon-scented bacon jam mixed with cream cheese to create an unexpectedly sweet and savory spread that would be lovely on Pumpkin Gruyère Muffins (Chapter 4), Sharp Cheddar Ale Muffins (Chapter 3), or Caramelized Onion and Bacon Muffins (Chapter 3).

Yields approximately 1½ cups

8 ounces thick-cut applewood-smoked bacon, cut into 1-inch pieces

½ large sweet onion, cut into ¼-inch thick slices

2 tablespoons light brown sugar

1 clove garlic, minced

¼ teaspoon allspice

¼ teaspoon cinnamon

Pinch freshly grated nutmeg

Pinch ground cloves

¼ teaspoon dry chipotle powder

¼ teaspoon smoked paprika

¼ cup espresso

2 tablespoons apple cider vinegar

¼ cup bourbon

2 tablespoons maple syrup

2 teaspoons hot sauce

½ cup cream cheese, at room temperature

1. In a large skillet over medium-high heat, cook the bacon pieces until they begin to crisp at the edges but are still soft in the centers, about 1–1½ minutes per side. Transfer the bacon to a paper towel–lined plate to drain. Pour all but 1 tablespoon of the bacon drippings from the pan.

2. Lower the heat to medium low and add the onion and brown sugar. Cook until the onions are well caramelized, about 20 minutes. Add the garlic, allspice, cinnamon, nutmeg, cloves, chipotle powder, and smoked paprika, and cook an additional 5 minutes to toast the spices and brown the garlic.

3. Add the espresso, apple cider vinegar, bourbon, maple syrup, hot sauce, and bacon to the pan. Increase the heat to medium and bring the mixture to a boil, then reduce the heat to low and simmer for about 2 hours, checking the mixture every 30 minutes. If the mixture becomes too dry, add a few tablespoons of water; you want the final mixture to be moist and very sticky but not runny.

4. Let the mixture cool slightly, then put it into the bowl of a food processor and pulse until roughly ground, about 20 times. Add the cream cheese, and pulse until well combined, about 10 pulses. Transfer to a serving bowl and chill for 1 hour, or up to 3 days, before serving.

CHAPTER 6

Crumbles and Glazes

Nothing makes an already pretty muffin look even more delectable than a golden brown crumble or a shiny, sweet glaze. But these toppings are not just for show. With gourmet ingredients such as fresh grated Parmesan cheese and smoky paprika, and unusual flavor combinations such as coconut milk and limoncello, these upscale toppings set the stage for equally upscale muffins. The options for toppings are almost endless, as varied as the muffins they go on. Add a layer of flavor to a peanut butter muffin with a butterscotch crumble, or a burst of tangy freshness to a coconut muffin with a lime glaze. No matter what you choose, the recipes in this chapter will help you dress your muffins up to impress with easy yet elegant crumbles and glazes!

Butterscotch Glaze

Butterscotch is basically a brown sugar caramel, but there is nothing basic about the flavor! Buttery and nutty, butterscotch has a complex flavor and aroma, and when used as a glaze it becomes a delicious adornment with immediate impact! This glaze works best on nutty or chocolaty muffins such as Brown Sugar Muffins (Chapter 1) or Spiced Nut Muffins (Chapter 4). But it can also be used on muffins that combine sweet and salty, especially muffins with chocolate and bacon like the Chocolate Chip and Candied Bacon Muffins in Chapter 4.

Yields enough glaze for 18 muffins

½ cup packed light brown sugar

1 tablespoon corn syrup

1 tablespoon water

3 tablespoons heavy cream

2 tablespoons butter

1 tablespoon whiskey or scotch

½ cup powdered sugar

1. In a medium saucepan with deep sides over medium-high heat, combine the brown sugar, corn syrup, and water. Brush down the sides of the pan with a wet pastry brush until the mixture begins to bubble.
2. Bring the mixture to a full boil and cook until it becomes very dark in color and smells like caramel, about 4 minutes. Remove the saucepan from the heat and carefully whisk in the cream, butter, and whiskey.
3. Allow the mixture to cool for 5 minutes. Then in the work bowl of a stand mixer, combine the brown sugar mixture with the powdered sugar. Beat until smooth. If the mixture is thick, add water ¼ teaspoon at a time until it thins out. Use immediately or cover and store at room temperature for up to 1 day.

Coconut Glaze

Coconut milk is the secret to the richness and amazing flavor of this glaze! Pressed from the flesh of fresh coconut, coconut milk has a mild coconut flavor and a creamy texture similar to that of heavy cream. This recipe combines the coconut milk with a little vanilla to help the exotic, fresh coconut flavor of the glaze really pop! For the best results use full-fat coconut milk here, not the light variety, which is more watery.

Yields enough glaze for 18 muffins

1 cup powdered sugar
2 tablespoons butter, melted and cooled
3 tablespoons coconut milk
1 teaspoon vanilla
¼ cup toasted coconut, for garnish

In a medium bowl combine the powdered sugar, butter, and 2 tablespoons of the coconut milk. Whisk, adding the final tablespoon of coconut milk a drop at a time until the glaze is the consistency of corn syrup. Add the vanilla and whisk well. Use immediately, sprinkling the toasted coconut over the wet glaze so it will stick to the muffin tops.

Streusel Crumble

This is a simple recipe, but it yields a crumble topping that is crisp, buttery, and bakes up a beautiful golden brown. The texture—and added flavor—that this recipe will add to muffins like the Cranberry Orange Streusel Muffins in Chapter 2, is well worth the few minutes it takes to make. Be sure to chill this crumble before adding it to the muffin batter for at least 10 minutes for maximum crispness.

Yields enough crumble for 18 muffins

½ cup all-purpose flour
½ cup sugar
⅛ teaspoon allspice
Pinch of salt
¼ cup butter, chilled

In a medium bowl combine the flour, sugar, allspice, and salt. Mix well, then add the butter and, with your fingers, rub the butter into the dry ingredients until the mixture looks clumpy and all the dry ingredients are coated with butter. Cover and chill for 10 minutes before use.

Orange Glaze

Fresh oranges, with their bright color and familiar flavor, are incredibly versatile. From simple juice to marinades, they can be used in a variety of applications. For this recipe the juice of the orange and the zest are both used to make a glaze that is loaded with bright orange goodness! But this glaze does more than just taste great. The little specs of bright orange zest in the glaze make for a beautiful and aromatic decoration! Try this on the exotic Cherry *Mahlab* Muffins or Orange Saffron Muffins in Chapter 1.

Yields enough glaze for 18 muffins

1 cup powdered sugar
2 tablespoons butter, melted and cooled
3 tablespoons freshly squeezed orange juice
1 tablespoon freshly grated orange zest
½ teaspoon vanilla

In a medium bowl combine the powdered sugar, butter, and 1 tablespoon of the orange juice. Whisk, adding more orange juice a drop at a time until the glaze is the consistency of corn syrup. Add the orange zest and vanilla, and whisk well. Use immediately or cover and store at room temperature for up to 1 day.

Limoncello Glaze

This pale yellow glaze is the perfect blend of sweet and sharp! Limoncello, an Italian lemon liqueur, is a tangy sweet drink that is popular in cocktails and as an apéritif. Here it is used to flavor a glaze perfect for muffins flavored with nuts, citrus, and fruit such as the Lemon Poppy Seed Muffins in Chapter 1. If you prefer, you could use orangecello, the orange version of the liqueur, or even plain citrus juice instead of the limoncello.

Yields enough glaze for 18 muffins

1 cup powdered sugar
2 tablespoons butter, melted and cooled
3 tablespoons limoncello
½ teaspoon vanilla
1 drop yellow food coloring

In a medium bowl combine the powdered sugar, butter, and 1 tablespoon of the limoncello. Whisk, adding more limoncello a drop at a time until the glaze is the consistency of corn syrup. Add the vanilla and food coloring, and whisk well. Use immediately or cover and store at room temperature for up to 1 day.

Limoncello Glaze with Lemon Poppy Seed Muffins (see Chapter 1)

Brown Sugar Streusel

Finely ground nuts and brown sugar make this delicious topping crisp and hearty! For the best results use nuts that complement the muffin such as ground pecans for Port Poached Pear Muffins in Chapter 1, or ground salted peanuts for Salted Peanut Crunch Muffins (Chapter 4). Because you can customize the flavor you could even use a blend of ground nuts to suit your taste!

Yields enough streusel for 18 muffins

½ cup all-purpose flour

½ cup packed light brown sugar

¼ cup finely ground nuts (almonds, peanuts, walnuts, or pecans)

Pinch of salt

¼ cup butter, chilled

In a medium bowl combine the flour, brown sugar, nuts, and salt. Mix well, then add the butter and, with your fingers, rub the butter into the dry ingredients until the mixture looks clumpy and all the dry ingredients are coated with butter. Cover and chill for 10 minutes before use.

Butterscotch Crumble

The caramel flavor that is inherent in brown sugar gives this pretty crumble some deep flavors—and this recipe uses browned butter to accentuate that richness. Combining the caramel of the brown sugar with the nutty flavors of brown butter creates an irresistible topping for muffins like Peanut Butter Butterscotch Crumb Muffins (Chapter 1)! If you want, a pinch of cardamom or nutmeg would also be lovely here.

Yields enough crumble for 18 muffins

¼ cup butter

½ cup all-purpose flour

½ cup packed light brown sugar

Pinch of salt

¼ teaspoon vanilla

1. In a small saucepan over medium heat, add the butter. Cook, stirring constantly, until the butter foams and turns a deep nut-brown color, about 12 minutes. Remove from the heat and cool to room temperature.

2. In a medium bowl combine the flour, brown sugar, and salt. Mix well, then add the butter and vanilla and, with your fingers, rub the butter into the dry ingredients until the mixture looks clumpy and all the dry ingredients are coated with butter. Cover and chill for 10 minutes before use.

Salted Caramel Glaze

Salted caramel has an almost magical quality to it. It is sweet and made sweeter by its salty bite. While you could easily just drizzle a little salted caramel directly on your muffins—which would be lovely—you can also whip it into a smooth, creamy glaze that can be used for dipping and drizzling on muffins like the Pumpkin Caramel Muffins in Chapter 1. Try doubling the caramel recipe as the extra is excellent as a garnish.

Yields enough glaze for 18 muffins

¼ cup sugar

2 teaspoons water

2 teaspoons corn syrup

3 tablespoons heavy cream

1 tablespoon butter

½ teaspoon sea salt

1 cup powdered sugar

½ teaspoon vanilla

2 tablespoons half-and-half

1. In a small saucepan with deep sides over medium-high heat, combine the sugar, water, and corn syrup. Brush down the sides of the pan with a wet pastry brush until the mixture begins to bubble.
2. Bring the mixture to a full boil and cook until it becomes dark amber in color and smells like caramel, about 6 minutes. Remove the saucepan from the heat and carefully whisk in the heavy cream, butter, and sea salt. Allow the caramel to cool to room temperature.
3. In a medium bowl combine the caramel with the powdered sugar, vanilla, and half-and-half. Whisk until smooth. Use immediately or cover and store at room temperature for up to 1 day.

Oat and Pecan Crumble on *Apple and Date Muffins (see Chapter 2)*

Oat and Pecan Crumble

Rolled oats are used two ways in the crumble to give maximum oat flavor: Whole oats are used, along with roughly chopped pecans, to provide texture and unaffected charm. Ground oats are mixed with the flour to add even more oat flavor, and to give the crumble a slight chewiness that is lovely with a tender muffin such as the Whole-Wheat Banana Pecan Muffins or the Apple and Date Muffins from Chapter 2!

Yields enough crumble for 18 muffins

⅓ cup all-purpose flour

2 tablespoons finely ground rolled oats

¼ cup sugar

¼ cup packed light brown sugar

⅓ cup finely chopped pecans

¼ cup rolled oats

¼ teaspoon cinnamon

Pinch of salt

⅓ cup butter, chilled

In a medium bowl combine the flour, ground oats, sugar, brown sugar, pecans, rolled oats, cinnamon, and salt. Mix well, then add the butter and, with your fingers, rub the butter into the dry ingredients until the mixture looks clumpy and all the dry ingredients are coated with butter. Cover and chill for 10 minutes before use.

Cinnamon Pecan Streusel

This recipe creates a rustic topping that adds a touch of homemade charm to your muffins. Don't think that this one is just for show! With warm cinnamon and buttery pecans, this topping adds a layer of extra flavor, too. While the muffins bake, the nuts in the streusel gently toast to tease out even more nutty aroma and flavor! Try it on Dulce de Leche Muffins (Chapter 1) or Brown Butter Spice Muffins (Chapter 4).

Yields enough streusel for 18 muffins

½ cup all-purpose flour

½ cup sugar

¼ cup finely chopped pecans

¼ teaspoon cinnamon

Pinch of salt

¼ cup butter, chilled

In a medium bowl combine the flour, sugar, pecans, cinnamon, and salt. Mix well, then add the butter and, with your fingers, rub the butter into the dry ingredients until the mixture looks clumpy and all the dry ingredients are coated with butter. Cover and chill for 10 minutes before use.

Cream Cheese Drizzle

Cream cheese frosting has a not-too-sweet flavor with a decided tang that is immensely popular on cakes. For this recipe the popular frosting becomes a not-too-sweet and tangy drizzle perfect for garnishing sweet muffins! This is good on most any sweet muffin, but is particularly nice over muffins flavored with a little spice such as the Carrot Spice Muffins in Chapter 1!

Yields enough drizzle for 18 muffins

3 ounces cream cheese, at room temperature

1 tablespoon butter, at room temperature

2 tablespoons half-and-half

¼ teaspoon vanilla-bean paste

⅓ cup powdered sugar

⅛ teaspoon cinnamon

1. In a medium bowl cream together the cream cheese and butter until smooth. Next add the half-and-half and vanilla-bean paste and beat until well combined.
2. Add the powdered sugar 1 tablespoon at a time until the mixture is the consistency of honey, runny but not too thick. Add the cinnamon and stir to combine. Use immediately.

Almond Brown Sugar Topping

A sparkling, sugary crust dotted with slivered almonds is what you get when you adorn your muffins with this beautiful topping! While the ingredients are simple, there is a magic transformation in the oven: The sugar melts slightly and forms a shatteringly crisp sugar crust. For the best results used slivered almonds. They will toast as the muffins bake and become a lovely golden color. Try this topping on Spiced Nut Muffins (Chapter 4) or Orange Almond Muffins (Chapter 2).

Yields enough topping for 18 muffins

¼ cup sugar

⅓ cup packed light brown sugar

½ cup slivered almonds

1 tablespoon butter, melted and cooled

In a medium bowl combine the sugar, brown sugar, almonds, and softened butter. Stir well until the sugar looks like wet sand, then cover and chill for 20 minutes before use.

Mocha Glaze

The bitter flavor of coffee and the warm flavor of chocolate are a very popular combination, and here they are used to make a sweet, sticky glaze for all kinds of muffins! For best results use natural cocoa powder in this glaze. Natural cocoa powder has a sweeter chocolate flavor that pairs better with the coffee. Try this glaze on Double Shot Espresso Muffins (Chapter 1).

Yields enough glaze for 18 muffins

1 cup powdered sugar

1 tablespoon cocoa powder

2 tablespoons butter, melted and cooled

3 tablespoons fresh-brewed coffee, at room temperature

½ teaspoon vanilla

In a medium bowl combine the powdered sugar, cocoa powder, softened butter, and 1 tablespoon of the coffee. Whisk, adding more coffee a drop at a time until the glaze is the consistency of corn syrup. Add the vanilla and whisk well. Use immediately or cover and store at room temperature for up to 1 day.

Peanut Butter Drizzle

Who can resist peanut butter? The roasty-toasty flavor and unmistakable scent of peanut butter is a crowd pleaser, and it is the star ingredient in this recipe! This pale buff-colored drizzle is the perfect adornment to any peanut butter muffin like the Peanut Butter Cream–Filled Banana Muffins in Chapter 1. Feel free to make this drizzle with other nut butters such as cashew, almond, and hazelnut if you're so inclined.

Yields enough drizzle for 18 muffins

¼ cup peanut butter

2 tablespoons butter, at room temperature

2 tablespoons half-and-half

¼ teaspoon vanilla

⅓ cup powdered sugar

1. In a medium bowl cream together the peanut butter and butter until smooth. Next add the half-and-half and vanilla, and beat until well combined.
2. Add the powdered sugar 1 tablespoon at a time until the mixture is the consistency of honey, runny but not too thick. Use immediately.

Minty Glaze

When it comes to mint, skip the extracts and go right to the source. Fresh mint is easy to find in most markets, and its rich, complex flavor makes it the secret ingredient in this glaze. Fresh mint syrup is easy to make at home, and the leftover syrup can be used to flavor iced tea and cocktails! Try this glaze on Peppermint White Chocolate Muffins (Chapter 1).

Yields enough glaze for 18 muffins

½ cup sugar
½ cup water
1 sprig fresh mint
1 cup powdered sugar
Pinch of salt
2 tablespoons butter, melted and cooled
2 tablespoons heavy cream
½ teaspoon vanilla

1. In a small saucepan combine the sugar, water, and mint. Place the mixture over medium heat and bring it just to a simmer. Once the sugar is completely dissolved, remove the pot from the heat and allow to cool to room temperature. Once cooled, remove the mint sprig and discard.
2. In a medium bowl combine the powdered sugar, salt, butter, and 2 tablespoons of the mint syrup. Whisk, adding the cream a drop at a time until the glaze is the consistency of corn syrup. Add the vanilla and whisk well. Use immediately or cover and store at room temperature for up to 1 day.

Vanilla Bean Icing

This icing is speckled with bits of little black vanilla beans, and these are what give it such a remarkable flavor. For this recipe you can use either prepared vanilla-bean paste, which is available in gourmet stores, or you can use the seeds scraped fresh from a vanilla pod. If possible, avoid vanilla extract, which, while nice, often lacks the pungency of vanilla beans. Try this icing on the Mascarpone Pound Cake Muffins in Chapter 1.

Yields enough icing for 18 muffins

1 cup powdered sugar
2 tablespoons butter, at room temperature
3 tablespoons half-and-half
Pinch of salt
½ teaspoon vanilla-bean paste

In a medium bowl combine the powdered sugar, butter, and 1 tablespoon of the half-and-half. Whisk, adding more half-and-half a drop at a time until the icing is thick and spreadable but not runny. Add the salt and vanilla-bean paste and whisk well. Use immediately or cover and store at room temperature for up to 1 day.

Vanilla Bean Icing on Mascarpone Pound Cake Muffins (see Chapter 1)

Cocoa Streusel

This topping is an unusual way to add a little chocolaty goodness to your muffins! Dutch-processed cocoa powder has a deeper, richer flavor and a darker color than natural cocoa powder and in this recipe it provides an instant hit of chocolate aroma and flavor. This streusel is wonderful on muffins like Chocolate Chocolate-Chip Spice Muffins (Chapter 4) or Rocky Road Streusel Muffins (Chapter 1), but give it a try on orange muffins for an unexpected twist.

Yields enough streusel for 18 muffins

⅓ cup all-purpose flour
2 tablespoons Dutch-processed cocoa powder
½ cup packed light brown sugar
¼ cup rolled oats
Pinch of salt
¼ cup butter, chilled

In a medium bowl combine the flour, cocoa, brown sugar, oats, and salt, and mix well. Add the butter and, with your fingers, rub the mixture until all the dry mixture is moistened and looks crumbly. Cover and chill 10 minutes before use.

Lemon Zest Streusel

How can you give your citrus muffins even more citrus flavor without resorting to a citrus glaze? Why, with this streusel, of course! Freshly grated lemon zest packs with it the essential oils of the lemon, and as it bakes those oils are released, giving this streusel a bright lemony smell. If you don't care for lemon, this recipe would also be lovely with orange or the more exotic Japanese yuzu! Try this refreshing streusel on the Blueberry Ricotta Streusel Muffins in Chapter 2.

Yields enough streusel for 18 muffins

½ cup all-purpose flour
1 tablespoon freshly grated lemon zest
½ cup sugar
Pinch of salt
¼ cup butter, chilled
1 teaspoon fresh lemon juice

In a medium bowl combine the flour, lemon zest, sugar, and salt, and mix well. Add the butter and lemon juice and, with your fingers, rub the mixture until all the dry mixture is moistened and looks crumbly. Cover and chill 10 minutes before use.

Oat Streusel

There are some flavors that just take you back and this recipe uses an oat topping that has all the flavor of Grandma's freshly baked oatmeal cookies! Subtle spices, rich dark brown sugar, and toasty oats make this streusel perfect for sweet muffins flavored with warm baking spices such as the Brown Butter and Oat Muffins from Chapter 2.

Yields enough streusel for 18 muffins

½ cup all-purpose flour
½ cup packed dark brown sugar
⅓ cup rolled oats
¼ teaspoon cinnamon
Pinch of nutmeg
Pinch of salt
¼ cup butter, chilled

In a medium bowl combine the flour, brown sugar, oats, cinnamon, nutmeg, and salt, and mix well. Add the butter and, with your fingers, rub the mixture until all the dry mixture is moistened and looks crumbly. Cover and chill 10 minutes before use.

Parmesan Crumble

Fresh Parmesan cheese has a sweetly nutty flavor and a pungent aroma. Like a good wine, Parmesan has different flavor characteristics based on where it is made and how long it has been aged. To find the best cheese, ask your cheese monger for samples and find the flavor you like best! Avoid the Parmesan that comes ready grated in cans and bags, as the flavor is dulled. Enjoy this crumble on the Pumpkin Gruyère Muffins in Chapter 4.

Yields enough crumble for 18 muffins

½ cup all-purpose flour
½ cup freshly grated Parmesan cheese
½ teaspoon Italian seasoning
¼ teaspoon salt
¼ cup butter, at room temperature

In a medium bowl combine the flour, Parmesan cheese, Italian seasoning, and salt, and mix well. Add the butter and, with your fingers, rub the mixture until all the dry mixture is moistened and looks crumbly. Cover and chill 20 minutes before use.

Savory Smoked Paprika Bacon Crumble

Crumbles are not just for sweet muffins; savory muffins like Caramelized Onion and Bacon Muffins (Chapter 3) can also be enhanced with a beautiful topping. For this unusual crumble, crisp cooked bacon is ground and combined with smoked paprika, cheese, and flaky panko bread crumbs to make something unexpectedly delicious.

Yields enough crumble for 18 muffins

4 strips thick-cut bacon, cooked very crisp

¼ cup panko bread crumbs

¼ cup all-purpose flour

½ teaspoon smoked paprika

¼ teaspoon salt

¼ cup butter, at room temperature

¼ cup finely shredded mild Cheddar cheese

1. In a blender or food processor, add the bacon and process until the bacon forms very fine crumbs.
2. In a medium bowl combine the ground bacon, panko bread crumbs, flour, smoked paprika, and salt, and mix well. Add the butter and cheese and, with your fingers, rub the mixture until all the dry mixture is moistened and looks crumbly. Cover and chill 20 minutes before use.

Index

About the Author

KELLY JAGGERS is a recipe developer, food blogger, and founder of EvilShenanigans.com, which was nominated for the Foodbuzz Blog Awards. She specializes in creating indulgent recipes that feature fresh, seasonal ingredients . . . and lots and lots of butter. Kelly, the author of *Not-So-Humble Pies* and *The Everything® Pie Cookbook*, has worked as a caterer and personal chef, and also creates wedding and specialty cakes. Her recipes have been featured in the *Food News Journal* and on the Cooking Club of America's website, and she is a member of The Learning Channel's Cake Crew. She lives in Dallas, Texas.